LECTURE READY 2

SECOND EDITION

PEG SAROSY
KATHY SHERAK

STRATEGIES FOR
Academic Listening and Speaking

OXFORD
UNIVERSITY PRESS

OXFORD
UNIVERSITY PRESS

198 Madison Avenue
New York, NY 10016 USA

Great Clarendon Street, Oxford, OX2 6DP, United Kingdom

Oxford University Press is a department of the University of Oxford.
It furthers the University's objective of excellence in research, scholarship,
and education by publishing worldwide. Oxford is a registered trade
mark of Oxford University Press in the UK and in certain other countries

General Manager, American ELT: Laura Pearson
Publisher: Stephanie Karras
Associate Publishing Manager: Sharon Sargent
Development Editor: Rebecca Mostov
Director, ADP: Susan Sanguily
Executive Design Manager: Maj-Britt Hagsted
Electronic Production Manager: Julie Armstrong
Designer: Debbie Lofaso
Production Artists: Julie Sussman-Perez, Elissa Santos
Image Manager: Trisha Masterson
Image Editor: Liaht Pashayan
Production Coordinator: Christopher Espejo

ISBN: 978 0 19 441728 0   LECTURE READY 2

Printed in China

This book is printed on paper from certified and well-managed sources

ACKNOWLEDGEMENTS

Illustrations by: Karen Minot, p55.

Commissioned photography by: Rogin Kim

*We would also like to thank the following for permission to reproduce the following
photographs*: Cover, Jan Greune/Getty Images, AP Photo/Franka Bruns; Frontmatter
cover reduction photo, © MARTIN RUETSCHI/Keystone/Corbis; Marcin Krygier/
iStockphoto (laptop); Ismail Akin Bostanci/istockphoto.com (iphone); p1 Purestock/
Getty Images; p2 James Hardy/Photoalto/Corbis UK Ltd.; p6 Photodisc/Oxford
University Press; p10 Image Source/Getty Images; p11 Photodisc/Oxford University
Press; p14 Stockbyte/Getty Images; p22 Tom Bonaventure/Getty Images; p27 Zero
Creatives/Getty Images; p28 PhotoAlto/Alamy; p29 Photodisc/Oxford University
Press (WORD); p29 David Young-Wolff/Alamy (WORD); p37 Somos/Oxford
University Press; p48 Tetra Images/Oxford University Press; p49 I love images/
Oxford University Press; p53 Horst Herget/Masterfile; p54 Randy Glasbergen; p62
Ariel Skelley/Oxford University Press; p63 Alexander Shalamov/Oxford University
Press; p66 Konstantin Sutyagin/Shutterstock; p67 Ariel Skelley/Getty Images; p74
Photodisc/Oxford University Press; p79 Leontura/Getty Images; p80 Iain Masterton/
Alamy; p86 CJG - Technology/Alamy; p88 Gareth Boden/Oxford University Press; p89
Blend Images/Oxford University Press; p92 c.20thC.Fox/Everett/Rex Features; p98
Moodboard/Oxford University Press; p99 Absodels/Getty Images; p101 Westend61/
Getty Images; p102 Image Source/Getty Images; p105 Rob Melnychuk/Getty Images;
p106 Leo Cullum/The Cartoon Bank; p107 Kevin Dodge/Corbis UK
Ltd.; p112 iStockphoto/Thinkstock; p114 Leontura/Getty Images;
p126 Image Source/Getty Images; p127 THIERRY CHARLIER/AFP/
Getty Images.

ACKNOWLEDGEMENTS

We would like to acknowledge the following individuals for their input during the development of the series:

ELLEN BARRETT
Wayne State University
Michigan, U.S.A.

DAVID BUNK
Portland State University
Oregon, U.S.A.

SAMANTHA BURNS
Dhofar University
Oman

SHIOW-WEN CHEN
Cheng Hsiu University
Kaohsiung

ELAINE COCKERHAM
Higher College of Technology
Oman

HITOSHI EGUCHI
Hokusei Gakuen University
Sapporo, Japan

TRACY FALCONER
University of Nebraska at Kearney
Nebraska, U.S.A.

JONATHAN FREEDMAN
Srinakharinwirot University
Bangkok, Thailand

JAMES HARMAN
Kanto Kokusai Koto Gakko
Tokyo, Japan

HASSAN HAWASH
Abu Dhabi Men's College
The United Arab Emirates

MARGARET LAYTON
University of Nevada
Nevada, U.S.A.

WILLIAM LITTLE
Georgetown University
Washington, DC, U.S.A.

JESSICA MATCHETT
Handong Global University
Pohang, South Korea

FERNANDA ORTIZ
CESL, University of Arizona
Arizona, U.S.A.

GABOR PINTER
Kobe University
Kobe, Japan

JOHN RACINE
Dokkyo University
Saitama, Japan

STEPHANIE STEWART
University of Houston
Texas, U.S.A.

WARUNWAN TANGSUWAN
Slipakorn University
Bangkok, Thailand

JAKCHAI YIMNGAM
Rajamangala University of Technology
Phra Nakhon
Bangkok, Thailand

LECTURE READY 2 CONTENTS

STUDENT BOOKS

iTOOLS FOR ALL LEVELS

GO ONLINE DIGITAL DOWNLOAD CENTER

Lecture Ready

- Prepares students for listening, note taking, and academic discussion through videos of realistic and engaging lectures.

- Explicit presentation skills prepare students for public speaking, a requirement in today's academic and professional world.

- Audio and video available through the Lecture Ready Digital Download Center, www.lectureready.com/student, allows students to study anytime, anywhere.

- Video-based assessment tracks progress to show what students have mastered and where they still need help.

Lecture Ready: Strategies for Academic Listening and Speaking guides students through the complete academic process.

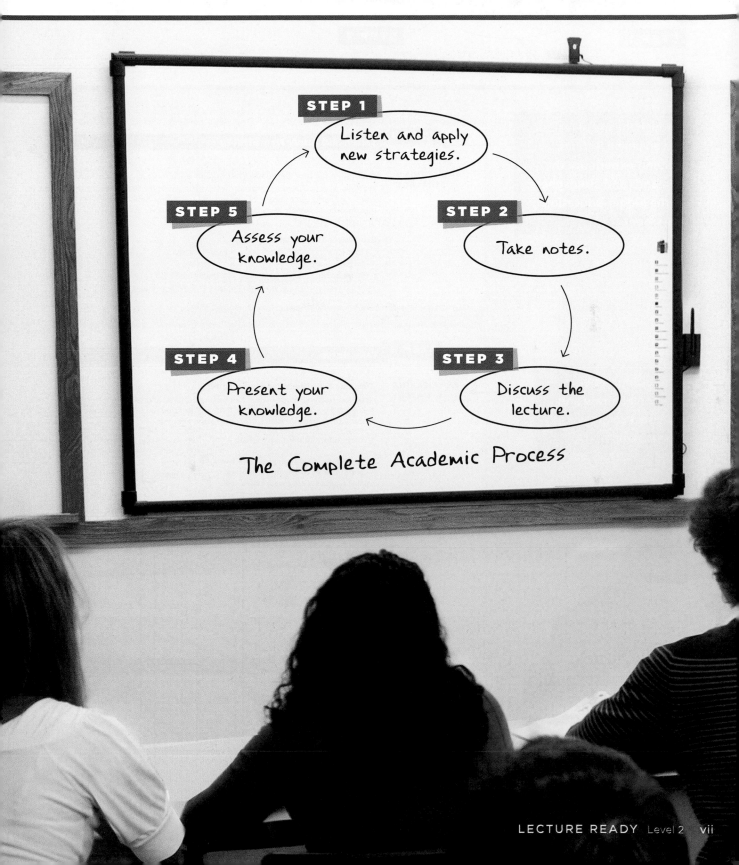

STEP 1
Listen and apply new strategies.

STEP 2
Take notes.

STEP 3
Discuss the lecture.

STEP 4
Present your knowledge.

STEP 5
Assess your knowledge.

The Complete Academic Process

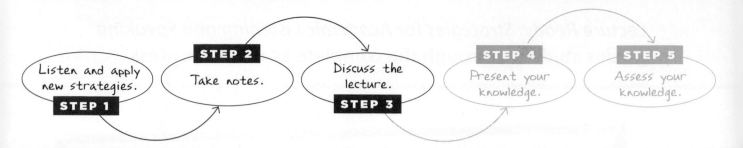

STEP 1 — Listen and apply new strategies.
STEP 2 — Take notes.
STEP 3 — Discuss the lecture.
STEP 4 — Present your knowledge.
STEP 5 — Assess your knowledge.

Through the use of realistic and engaging lectures, students **experience the demands and atmosphere of the higher-education classroom.**

STEP 1 — Listen and Apply New Strategies

LISTENING STRATEGY

Recognize Lecture Language That Signals a Definition
Professors often use new words as they explain new information or ideas. They also use a variety of expressions to present definitions for those words. Listen for the words and expressions that professors use to signal a definition.

Expressions That Signal a Definition
- that is, . . .
- in other words, . . .
- X, meaning . . .
- by X, I mean . . .
- X means . . .
- What I mean by X is . . .

Another common signal for a definition is a rhetorical question.

Note-taking strategies focus on **accurate and concise** recording of class material.

STEP 2 — Take Notes

NOTE-TAKING STRATEGY

Describe the Visuals Used in a Lecture
Professors often include visuals like pictures, charts, and graphs in lectures to clarify ideas. Make sure that you describe the visual in your notes and write down important information about it.

Excerpt and Visual from a Lecture

You breathe in through your nose and mouth. The air travels down through a large tube in your throat called the windpipe. Then it moves through large and small tubes in your lungs called bronchial tubes or airways. The airways in your lungs look something like an upside-down tree with many branches.

bronchial tubes and alveoli

Representation of Visual in Notes

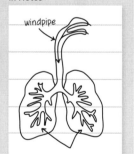
windpipe

Academic discussion strategies **help students participate fully and smoothly** in classroom discussions.

STEP 3 — Discuss the Lecture

ACADEMIC DISCUSSION STRATEGY

Connect Your Ideas to Other Students' Ideas
During a discussion, you may have an idea that is related to something that someone else said. Use expressions to show that you understand how these ideas are connected and that you want to add your idea to the discussion.

Expressions for Connecting Your Ideas to Others' in a Discussion
- My idea is similar to Sam's.
- I disagree with what Sam said.

STEP 1 — Listen and apply new strategies.
STEP 2 — Take notes.
STEP 3 — Discuss the lecture.
STEP 4 — Present your knowledge.
STEP 5 — Assess your knowledge.

STEP 4 — Present Your Knowledge

PRESENTATION STRATEGY

Use Hand Gestures to Clarify Words and Ideas

The words a speaker uses in a presentation convey the most meaning. However, effective hand gestures can enhance the meaning of the words and ideas. Gestures can also help the audience recognize when an idea is important.

Use your hands to enhance what you're saying and to emphasize important ideas.

> Students are more competent and confident when they learn **how to present** using proven strategies for academic success.

Check your comprehension

GO ONLINE

A. Watch a student give a presentation about stereotypes on television. Then answer these two questions.

1. What group of people does the student discuss?

_____

2. What is the student's opinion of television's portrayal of this group?

_____

> These strategies help students meet their presentation challenges in and **beyond the language classroom.**

ce hand gestures

GO ONLINE

B. Watch the video again. Think about the information in the strategy box above. In your notebook, list two problems with the student's hand gestures.

GO ONLINE

C. The student received some suggestions about his presentation and delivered it again. Watch the new presentation. In your notebook, list two improvements the student made to his hand gestures.

> **Videos of presentations for each presentation strategy** allow students to see and apply these skills to their own presentations.

STEP 1
Listen and apply new strategies.

STEP 2
Take notes.

STEP 3
Discuss the lecture.

STEP 4
Present your knowledge.

STEP 5
Assess your knowledge.

Video-based tests track progress to show what students have mastered and where they still need help.

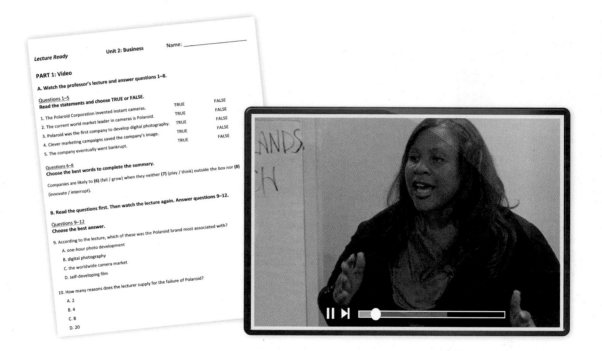

Lecture Ready Unit 2: Business Name: _____

PART 1: Video

A. Watch the professor's lecture and answer questions 1–8.

Questions 1–5
Read the statements and choose TRUE or FALSE.

1. The Polaroid Corporation invented instant cameras. TRUE FALSE
2. The current world market leader in cameras is Polaroid. TRUE FALSE
3. Polaroid was the first company to develop digital photography. TRUE FALSE
4. Clever marketing campaigns saved the company's image. TRUE FALSE
5. The company eventually went bankrupt. TRUE FALSE

Questions 6–8
Choose the best words to complete the summary.

Companies are likely to (6) (fail / grow) when they neither (7) (play / think) outside the box nor (8) (innovate / interrupt).

B. Read the questions first. Then watch the lecture again. Answer questions 9–12.

Questions 9–12
Choose the best answer.

9. According to the lecture, which of these was the Polaroid brand most associated with?
   A. one-hour photo development
   B. digital photography
   C. the worldwide camera market
   D. self-developing film

10. How many reasons does the lecturer supply for the failure of Polaroid?
   A. 2
   B. 4
   C. 8
   D. 20

GO ONLINE **Lecture Ready Assessment Program**

Unit, midterm, and final exams can be found on iTools or www.lectureready.com/teacher.

- **CUSTOMIZABLE** Adapt tests to meet the precise needs of students.

- **EFFECTIVE** Prepare student for standardized tests.

- **ENGAGING** All tests are based on **100% NEW video content**.

Lecture Ready Student Resources

CONNECT

Downloadable video and audio allow students to study **anytime, anywhere**.

ENGAGE

Students fully engage in the learning experience by **downloading and watching** each chapter's lecture and student presentation models.

ASSESS

Video-based unit, midterm, and final exams allow ongoing assesment.

Lecture Ready

Watch the lecture and then answer questions 1–4.

Questions 1–2
Fill in the blanks in the outline below. Write one word in each blank.

Primary Goals of Psychology
A. to observe and describe behavior
B. (1.) to_____ behavior
C. to predict behavior
D.(2.) to_____ behavior

Questions 3–4: Choose the best answer for each question.
3. According to the lecture, why is it difficult to explain people's behavior?
A. Many people try to hide their behavior.
B. There is often not enough time to observe behavior.
C. Behavior depends in part on culture.

4. According to the lecture, how do psychologists usually make predictions?
A. by discussing people's past behavior
B. by performing experiments
C. by reading about people's behavior

Watch Again
Watch the lecture a second time. Then answer questions 5–10.

 **ONLINE**

IT'S EASY! Use the access code printed on the inside back cover of this book to download video and audio at www.lectureready.com/student.

Lecture Ready iTools bring the book, video, and audio together in one classroom presentation tool.

- For use with an LCD projector or interactive whiteboard
- Full student book for in-class viewing
- All video and audio links at point of use for whole-class presentations
- Unit, midterm, and final tests based on 100% NEW additional video content available as click-and-print PDFs and customizable Word documents
- Answer Keys and Teaching Notes

Teacher Digital Download Center

Go to www.lectureready.com/teacher. See your local representative to order a Teacher Resource Access Code.

For additional support email our customer support team at **eltsupport@oup.com**.

Unit Goals

Marketing

marketing \\ˈmɑrkətɪŋ\\ The study of the processes and techniques involved with promoting, selling, and distributing a product or service

CHAPTER 1

Learn about differences in how men and women spend money and how this affects marketing

Listening Strategies

- Build background knowledge to understand lectures
- Recognize lecture language that signals the topic
- Use background knowledge to predict lecture content

Note-Taking Strategies

- Write down the most important words in a lecture
- Assess and revise your notes after a lecture

Academic Discussion Strategy

- Enter the discussion and participate actively

Presentation Strategy

- Make eye contact with the audience while using notes

CHAPTER 2

Learn about the reasons behind recent changes in advertising

Listening Strategy

- Recognize lecture language that signals the big picture of a lecture

Note-Taking Strategies

- Use an informal outline to organize your notes
- Summarize the lecture

Academic Discussion Strategy

- Contribute ideas to the discussion

Presentation Strategy

- Catch the audience's attention by telling a story

STEP 1

Listen and Apply New Strategies

LISTENING STRATEGY

Build Background Knowledge to Understand Lectures

Before you go to a lecture, think about what you already know about the lecture's topic. Complete any reading assignments, and discuss your reading with classmates. This will give you necessary background information and vocabulary that will prepare you to take in new information in the lecture.

Think about the topic

A. Look at the picture of a husband and wife shopping together. Then work with a partner to do the exercise below.

Imagine this situation. A husband and wife go together to a big department store. The store has a wide variety of products—clothes, computers, food, appliances, automotive supplies, and furniture. The couple decide to separate and meet again in an hour.

1. What things do you think the man will shop for?

2. What things do you think the woman will shop for?

3. In the same situation, what would you probably shop for? Do you think your shopping habits are typical? Why or why not?

B. Read this article about the changing shopping habits of women.

Women Enter the Electronics Market

Just as men and women's roles and responsibilities are changing in society, so are the shopping habits of the two **genders**. The electronics industry (computers, cell phones, digital cameras, etc.) is one place where gender differences in purchasing are rapidly changing.

Until very recently, the electronics **market** consisted mostly of men. Today, however, women are some of the biggest **consumers** of computers and other electronics. With more and more women working and in control of their own and their family's money, women now want **to have a say in** the type of electronics that they have in their homes. Some experts report that women are actually buying more electronics than men. A recent **study** by the Consumer Electronics Association reports another interesting development. It states that almost a third of the new and more **innovative** electronics are sold to women. So not only are women becoming more interested in electronics purchases in general, but they are also increasingly willing to try the latest products.

Women are now spending more than $50 billion on electronics. What are the **implications** of this change in women's spending habits for marketing? Laura Heller, senior editor of *DSN Retailing Today*, believes that until recently women have been

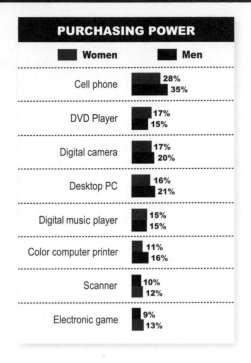

PURCHASING POWER

	Women	Men
Cell phone	28%	35%
DVD Player	17%	15%
Digital camera	17%	20%
Desktop PC	16%	21%
Digital music player	15%	15%
Color computer printer	11%	16%
Scanner	10%	12%
Electronic game	9%	13%

ignored by the electronics industry. She says, "There's so much we don't know about this group: How they shop for electronics, how they feel about these products, and more importantly, how these products make them feel." Businesses need to understand the changes in their customer population and create new **strategies** to meet consumers' needs. These strategies will focus on the need to **appeal** to their new customers—women.

C. Answer these questions about the article. Then discuss your answers
with a partner.

1. What is one change in the way women spend money?

_____

2. What's one interesting development in the electronics industry today?

_____

3. What questions do electronics marketers have about women?

_____

D. Match the words with their definitions. Look back at the article on page
3 to check your answers.

___	1. gender	**a.**	a person who buys things or uses services
___	2. market	**b.**	to be attractive or interesting to someone
___	3. consumer	**c.**	developed using new ways of thinking
___	4. study	**d.**	plan used to achieve a goal
___	5. innovative	**e.**	a research project about a particular subject
___	6. implication	**f.**	classification of people as male or female
___	7. strategy	**g.**	the effect that something will have in the future
___	8. appeal	**h.**	the demand for product; those people who desire a product

E. Circle the phrase with a similar meaning to the underlined idiom.

Women today are more involved in family finances, so they also want
<u>to have a say in</u> purchasing decisions for the home.

a. to tell someone about
b. to be part of
c. to make

F. Discuss these questions in a group. Share your answers with the class.

1. Think of the men and women that you know. What changes have you
noticed in their shopping interests? Give some examples.

2. Think of a store that usually appeals to men. What could it do to appeal
to women? What could a "woman's" store do to appeal to men?

G. With a partner, discuss three things that you have learned from the reading and from your discussion about gender and spending.

1. _____

2. _____

3. _____

H. To help you understand the listening strategy, work with a partner to discuss the situation below and to answer the question.

You arrive five minutes late to class, and the professor has already begun the lecture. You start to take notes, even though you are not sure what the lecture is about. You see that the student next to you understands the lecture. What is one quick question you can ask your classmate to help you get oriented to the professor's lecture?

**LISTENING
STRATEGY**

Recognize Lecture Language for the Topic

Often when students come to a university lecture, they have a lot of background information about the topic from the reading that they've done for homework. However, when the professor begins the lecture, students don't know exactly what the lecture will be about. At the beginning of a lecture, the professor usually tells you the topic, or what the lecture is going to be about.

Listen for the words and expressions that professors use to tell you the topic.

Expressions That Signal the Topic of a Lecture
- Our topic today is . . .
- I'll be talking about . . .
- What I want to talk about today is . . .
- We'll be discussing . . .
- We're going to look at . . .
- Let's go back to our discussion of . . .
- Let's continue our discussion of . . .

I. Work with a partner to think of other expressions that signal the topic of a lecture. Write your examples here.

_____

_____

_____

Recognize topic lecture language

J. Read these introductions to two business lectures. Then underline and label the lecture language that signals the topic.

> Let's get started because the topic is really interesting. What I want to talk about is how people spend money. This is a really popular topic because everyone has a personal story about spending money.

All right. Are we ready? I want to look in depth at the chapter you read for homework. I want you to understand more about this topic, so we're going to look at the impact women have on the electronics market.

Listen to the lectures

GO ONLINE

K. Listen to the introductions of three different lectures. Write down the topic lecture language and the topic.

1. Topic lecture language: _____

_____

Topic: _____

2. Topic lecture language: _____

_____

Topic: _____

3. Topic lecture language: _____

_____

Topic: _____

NOTE-TAKING STRATEGY

Write the Most Important Words

During a lecture, you do not have time to write down every word that a professor says. Write down only the words that have the most meaning in the lecture.

The words that are **not** important to the meaning of the professor's ideas are usually in these categories:

pronouns: *our, my, their . . .*   **prepositions:** *in, on, at . . .*

helping verbs: *be, have, do . . .*   **conjunctions:** *and, but, so . . .*

determiners: *a, the, this . . .*

Write the most important words

A. Read this excerpt from a lecture on how men spend money. Then look at one student's notes from the lecture. Cross out the words in the lecture that are not in the notes. The first sentence has been done for you.

~~Our~~ topic is trends ~~in~~ gender ~~and~~ spending. New trends are in the electronics industry. Marketers and advertisers want to know the kinds of electronics women are buying and the electronic products men are buying.

Topic – trends gender/spending
New trends electronics industry
Marketers/advertisers want to know —
kinds electronics women buy/men buy

B. Read these sentences from a lecture on trends in spending. Write down only the words that have the most meaning in the lecture.

1. In the past, the electronics market consisted mostly of men.

_____

2. Almost a third of the new and more innovative electronics are being sold to women.

_____

3. Businesses have only recently noticed the change in their customer base and are beginning to create new strategies to appeal to women.

_____

Use Your Background Knowledge to Predict the Lecture's Content

To help you get ready for new information and listen more actively, think about what the professor might discuss in the lecture. Make a prediction based on what you already know.

Make predictions

C. Before the lecture, think about everything you have learned and discussed on the topic of gender and spending. What do you expect to learn from the lecture? Write three predictions below. Compare your predictions with a partner.

1. ___I expect to learn more about . . ._____

2. _____

3. _____

Watch the lecture

GO ONLINE

D. Watch the lecture, and take notes. Remember to write down the most important words. Listen for the lecture language that signals the topic.

Topic:

Traditional responsibilities for women

Traditional responsibilities for men

Changes to traditional roles

Changes in spending

Meaning for business

Marketing to women

E. Check the statement that best describes how well you were able to
recognize the lecture language.

___ I was able to recognize when the lecturer said the topic.

___ I didn't recognize when the lecturer said the topic.

F. Use your notes to answer these questions.

1. Traditionally, what types of things were women responsible for buying?

_____

_____

_____

2. Traditionally, what types of things were men responsible for buying?

_____

_____

_____

3. What are two reasons for the change in women's shopping habits?

_____

_____

_____

4. What are businesses doing to become female friendly?

_____

_____

_____

Assess and Revise Your Notes

During a lecture, you can sometimes miss an important idea or piece
of information. Compare notes with classmates in a study group after
the lecture to check that your notes are complete. Revise your notes.

G. Were you able to answer the questions in Exercise F using the
information in your notes? Compare and discuss your notes with a few
other students. Help each other fill in any missing information. Revise
your notes.

ACADEMIC DISCUSSION STRATEGY

Enter the Discussion

You will often be asked to discuss the lecture's ideas with the whole class or with a group of classmates. In these discussions, professors expect all students to participate actively. Do not wait for someone to ask you to speak. Instead, use expressions to enter the discussion so that you can contribute your ideas.

Expressions for Entering the Discussion

- I'd like to say something here.
- I'd like to comment on that.
- Can I say something here?
- Can I add something to that?
- I have a question about that.
- I'd like to add my two cents.

Note: Speakers often say a small word or interjection to get attention before using one of the expressions above.

- Well, I'd like to say something here.
- Yes, I have a question about that.
- So, can I say something here?
- Um, I'd like to add my two cents.

List more examples

A. Work with a partner to think of other expressions for entering a discussion. Write your examples here.

_____

_____

_____

B. In a group, read and discuss the questions below. Keep the conversation going until every student has had a chance to practice entering the discussion. Use your own ideas or the ones given below.

1. Where do women like to shop?

Possible Ideas
Stores that:
  are small
  have clear signs
  have nice lighting
  have helpful clerks

2. Where do men like to shop?

Possible Ideas
Stores that:
  are on the Internet
  have a variety of products
  have quick service
  have knowledgeable clerks

C. Discuss these ideas with your classmates. Remember to use the phrases for entering the discussion.

1. The professor pointed out that more and more women are making "big ticket" purchases such as computers and cars. Do you think this is true? Have you seen evidence of this change in spending habits?

2. According to the lecture, marketers are now trying to appeal more to women. Do you think marketers need to use different marketing strategies for men and for women?

3. If you were a marketing manager, how would you increase the appeal of a computer store (or car repair shop or hardware store) to women? How would you increase the appeal of a home decoration store (or supermarket or day spa) to men?

4. Look back at your notes. What was another idea in the lecture that you found important or interesting? Tell the class why you think it is important or interesting, and ask for their opinions.

PRESENTATION STRATEGY

Make Eye Contact while Using Notes

Looking at the audience during a presentation helps the audience stay interested and, as a result, better able to follow the speaker's ideas. This isn't always easy to do, especially when the speaker uses notes. It's important for the speaker to look down at his or her notes only briefly and spend more time looking at the audience.

Make eye contact with your audience to help them stay interested and follow your ideas.

Check your comprehension

GO ONLINE

A. Watch a student give a presentation about a marketing plan. Then answer these two questions.

1. According to the presenter, what are two problems with computer stores?

   _____

   _____

2. According to the presenter, what is one important thing marketers should know about children?

   _____

   _____

Notice eye contact

GO ONLINE

B. Watch the video again. Think about the information in the strategy box above. List two problems with the student's eye contact.

   _____

   _____

   _____

GO ONLINE **C.** The student received some suggestions about the presentation and delivered it again. Watch the new presentation. List two improvements the student made to her eye contact to keep the audience interested.

   _____

   _____

   _____

Strategies for Making Effective Eye Contact while Using Notes

- Establish eye contact with your audience before you begin speaking.
- Look down at your notes to remember what you want to say. Then look up when you say it.
- Move your head around so you can make eye contact with everyone in the room, not just the people in the front row.

List more examples

D. Work with a partner to think of other ways to make eye contact that keeps the audience interested. Write your examples here.

_____

_____

_____

Practice making eye contact

E. Work in a group. Choose one of the new words you have learned in this chapter. On a notecard, write the word, its definition, and its importance to marketing.

Stand in front of the group. Present the information on the notecard. As you speak, look at your notes briefly, and make eye contact with each person for three seconds.

After you finish, have your classmates give you feedback on your eye contact. Ask them these two questions:

1. What are two ways I made effective eye contact?

2. What is one way to improve my eye contact?

Give a presentation

F. Prepare and deliver a presentation about how a store can appeal to consumers.

Choose a store in your area that sells a specific product, such as computers, clothing, books, or tools.

Next, choose a specific group of consumers such as children, parents, elderly people, students, workers, or young people.

Analyze the target group of consumers, and explain how to design the store and train the workers to appeal to this group. Use the strategies for making eye contact.

Before you prepare your presentation, review the ideas and vocabulary from this chapter.

STEP 1 Listen and Apply New Strategies

Think about the topic   **A.** Look at the picture. Then with a partner discuss the questions below.

1. How many advertisements can you see in the photograph?

2. How many advertisements do you think you see in a typical day? Trace your steps and list the places where you see ads.

3. Do you think you see more ads now than you saw ten years ago? Why or why not?

4. What types of ads do you see today that you didn't see when you were a child?

B. Students in a Principles of Marketing course had to write a report about all of the advertising they encountered in a single day. Read one student's blog about his experiences with advertising.

Hiding in Plain Sight: Ads in Daily Life

I have to admit that I thought Professor Kinney's assignment was silly. What could I possibly learn from counting all the ads I see? But actually, it was really interesting. I always knew there was a lot of advertising out there—companies are in business to sell their **products**, so that's okay. But I couldn't believe all the ads "hidden in plain sight." I didn't realize just how many ads I see all around me every day but never notice. Here are some examples.

Yesterday morning I ran into the cafe on the ground floor of my dormitory to get some coffee. The server handed me a giant cup. I wasn't surprised to see that the cup advertised the cafe. The cup had a thick paper ring around it to protect my hand from the coffee's heat. On the ring, I noticed the **logo** of my favorite radio station. A radio station? On a coffee cup??? Was that there yesterday? It probably was.

I went outside and sat down on a bench to enjoy my liquid breakfast. There was an ad on the bench for an insurance company. The other benches had ads on them, too. I never noticed that before!

After class, I headed to the college bookstore. There's an electronic sign over the entrance flashing the word "Igneous." This word has nothing to do with books. Instead, it is the **brand name** of some cool bicycles I've seen around campus. Okay, I can understand that. College students ride bikes, so from the company's **perspective**, it makes sense to **promote** their products in a college bookstore.

From there I walked to my bank to get some money from the automatic teller machine (ATM). While I was waiting for the cash to come out, a five-second commercial for a new sports car played on the screen of the ATM. I really don't know how **cost-effective** that kind of ad is. I mean, it must be expensive to make, and I don't think the students here can even dream of buying a car like that. I wondered about the commercial, though. Did the machine wait until the commercial was over before it gave me my cash? Or is the length of the commercial made to fit the time that you have to wait for your cash anyway?

Well, I saw at least four ads, and I didn't even watch TV or read a magazine. Some of these ads seem traditional, like the ad painted on the bench. But some, like the ATM ad, were **high-tech**—they really use the latest **technology** to grab people's attention. I'm just not sure if the high-tech ads are more effective **in the long run** than the more traditional ads. Why make the ad so high-tech? I mean, you really can't look anywhere but the ATM screen while you're waiting for your cash, right? But would advertisers produce those ads if they didn't increase sales?

Lots of questions to bring up in my report! More on this later.

C. With a partner, discuss these questions about the reading.

1. What surprised the student about this assignment?

2. What kinds of ads did he see in one day? Where were they?

3. What questions occurred to him as he thought about his experience?

D. Circle the answer that correctly completes the definition of the word. Look back at the reading on page 15 to check your answers.

1. A <u>product</u> is something that is usually made in a ___.

   a. factory   **b.** shopping mall

2. A <u>logo</u> is ___ of a company.

   a. the symbol   **b.** the product

3. A <u>brand name</u> is the name that a company gives to its own ___.

   a. products   **b.** advertisements

4. <u>Perspective</u> refers to the way a person ___ something.

   a. thinks about   **b.** earns

5. To <u>promote</u> a product, a company ___ the product and hopes that people buy it.

   a. makes   **b.** advertises

6. An ad is <u>cost-effective</u> if a company ___ from it than the ad cost to produce.

   a. earns less money   **b.** earns more money

7. A <u>high-tech</u> company uses a lot of ___ equipment.

   a. modern   **b.** tall

8. <u>Technology</u> refers to all the machines or equipment used to ___ products.

   a. make   **b.** name

E. Circle the answer with a similar meaning to the underlined idiom.

High-tech ads may cost a company a lot of money to produce, but <u>in the long run</u>, they increase sales and company profits.

a. very quickly   **b.** sometimes   **c.** over a long time

Discuss the reading

F. Discuss these questions in a group. Share your answers with the class.

1. Do you think the number and placement of ads that the student saw is unusual? Why or why not?

2. How do you feel about ads that are "hidden in plain sight"?

3. Why do you think advertisers use these kinds of ads?

Review what you know

G. With a partner, discuss three things that you have learned from the reading and from your discussion about advertising.

1. _____

2. _____

3. _____

LISTENING STRATEGY

Recognize Lecture Language That Signals the Big Picture

You learned that a professor usually tells you the topic at the beginning of a lecture. A professor will often also give you the big picture, or the general plan of the lecture. The big picture is an overview of how the professor will present the material, like a map of the lecture.

Listen for the words and expressions that professors use to indicate the big picture.

Expressions That Signal the Big Picture of a Lecture

• First, we'll look at . . ., and then we'll move on to look at . . .
• I'm going to give you a few examples of . . .
• What I want to do today is discuss the causes of . . .
• We'll look at several ways that . . .
• I want to give you some background on . . .

List more examples

H. Work with a partner to think of other expressions that signal the big picture of a lecture. Write your examples here.

_____

_____

_____

I. Read each lecture introduction. Circle the topic. Then underline and label the lecture language that signals the topic and the big picture.

Lecture 1

Good afternoon. It's nice to see you all. It looks like you are ready to go, so let's get started. We'll be talking about techniques that advertisers use to sell movies. Think about the last movie you saw. Got it? Do you remember what made you go see the movie? OK. Well, this afternoon, we'll look at several ways that the movie industry advertises to movie-goers.

Lecture 2

Hi, everyone. Please take your seats so we can get started. Great. In today's lecture we're going to look at how high-tech products are advertised. To help you understand how sophisticated these ads are, I want to give you some background on the products and the education level of the people who use them.

Listen to the lectures

GO ONLINE

J. Listen to the introductions of three different lectures. First, listen to each introduction, and write down the topic. Then listen to the introductions again, and write down the big picture lecture language.

1. Topic: _____

_____

Big picture lecture language: _____

_____

2. Topic: _____

_____

Big picture lecture language: _____

_____

3. Topic: _____

_____

Big picture lecture language: _____

_____

NOTE-TAKING STRATEGY

Use an Informal Outline

Your notes should give you an accurate record of the ideas in the lecture and show you how different points are related to each other. Organizing your notes in an outline form—using indentation—helps you remember which information is most important and which information is related but less important such as examples, definitions, and dates.

Excerpt from a Lecture and Outline

Now I want to talk about the three ways that advertisers appeal to consumers. They use facts, statistics, and research reports. A typical example of a research report is the ad where you see the doctor who says that a pill will help decrease pain by 23 percent.

> 3 ways advertisers appeal to consumers
>
> facts
>
> statistics
>
> research reports
>
> typical example: doctor in ad says
>
> pill decreases pain 23%

Analyze the notes   **A.** Answer the questions about the excerpt and outline.

1. What is the topic in this part of the lecture? How does the student indicate this in his/her notes?

   _____

   _____

2. What are the three ways that advertisers appeal to people? How does the student indicate this?

   _____

   _____

3. Why is "typical example" indented under "research reports"?

   _____

   _____

B. Read this excerpt from a lecture on advertising. Take notes in outline form in your notebook.

> Let's move on to discuss emotional appeals in advertising. Emotional appeals are advertising messages that try to create a feeling about a product. You might see an emotional appeal in an ad for a product that makes the person feel happy. A good example of this is the soft drink ad that shows people laughing and having a great time . . . and we see someone who is holding the soft drink. Another example of that is a car ad that shows a well-dressed person driving an expensive car through beautiful scenery. This makes you feel wealthy and powerful. With both of these ads, you begin to have a good feeling about the product, . . . and the advertisers think maybe you'll go out and buy that product.

C. Before the lecture, think about everything you have learned and discussed on the topic of advertising. What do you expect to learn from the lecture? Write three predictions in your notebook. Compare your predictions with a partner.

D. Watch the lecture, and take notes using an informal outline. Remember to listen for the lecture language that signals the big picture.

Topic

New kinds of advertising

   One new kind of advertising

   Another new kind of advertising

Reasons ads are everywhere

   From advertiser's perspective

   Reasons for increase in advertising

E. Check the statement that best describes how well you were able to recognize the lecture language.

____ I was able to recognize when the lecturer said the big picture.

____ I didn't recognize when the lecturer said the big picture.

F. Use your notes to answer these questions. Write your answers in your notebook.

1. What are the two new kinds of ads explained in the lecture? Give one example of each new kind of ad.

2. What are the advantages of "hidden" ads for advertisers?

3. What are some reasons for the increase in advertising?

4. What is an example of how technology has contributed to the rise in advertising?

Use Your Notes to Summarize the Lecture

A good way to remember a lecture is to put the key ideas into your own words. This will also help you confirm that you understood all the information and that your notes are complete.

As soon as possible after a lecture, put the key ideas into your own words, and speak them out loud to a study partner or to yourself.

Imagine this situation: Your friend had to miss class because he was ill. The next day, he asks you to tell him about the lecture. What would you tell him?

You would probably give him the following information:
- the topic of the lecture
- the big picture of the lecture (the most important ideas)
- a few important points and examples

This is the same information that you use when you summarize.

Expressions for Summarizing

- The professor talked about . . .
- Then he discussed . . .
- She explained . . .
- He gave us the example of . . .
- She told us . . .
- After that he wrapped up with . . .

G. Work with a partner, and take turns. Review your notes from the lecture. Then summarize the main points of the lecture for your partner. Talk for 2–3 minutes only.

ACADEMIC DISCUSSION STRATEGY

Contribute to the Discussion

You can contribute your ideas throughout a discussion. Your ideas might be important or interesting points from the lecture, comments and observations about the topic, or your own opinions. Use expressions to show that you want to contribute something to the discussion.

Expressions for Contributing to the Discussion

- I think it was interesting that . . .
- I noticed that . . .
- I was wondering if . . .
- . . . is a good example of . . .

- I think . . .
- In my opinion, . . .
- To me, . . .
- . . . is really important because . . .

List more examples

A. Work with a partner to think of other expressions for contributing to a discussion. Write your examples here.

_____

_____

_____

B. In a group, read and discuss the questions below. Keep the conversation going until every student has had a chance to practice contributing to the discussion. Use your own ideas or the ones given below.

1. In a typical day, where do you see advertisements?

   Possible Ideas
   on buses
   on the Internet
   on park benches

2. What kinds of ads are you most likely to read or listen to?

   Possible Ideas
   ads for sports equipment
   ads for movies
   ads for electronics

3. What kinds of ads do you enjoy looking at?

   Possible Ideas
   humorous ads
   ads with celebrities
   ads for products I'm planning to buy

C. Discuss these ideas with your classmates. Remember to use the phrases for contributing ideas to the discussion.

1. The professor talked about ads that don't seem like ads. What other examples of this kind of advertising have you seen? Why do companies use "hidden ads"? How do you feel about them?

2. In the United States, there are restrictions on the placement of certain types of advertising. For example, cigarettes cannot be advertised on television. Is it fair that the advertising for some products is restricted? Why or why not? What types of products probably have restrictions on their advertising? Why?

3. Imagine that your company wants to advertise at a baseball stadium. You can choose to have a painted sign on the back fence or an electronic ad that will appear only on television. Which type of ad would you suggest? Why?

4. Look back at your notes. What was another idea in the lecture that you found important or interesting? Tell the class why you think it is important or interesting, and ask for your classmates' opinions.

PRESENTATION STRATEGY

Catch the Audience's Attention by Telling a Story

Beginning a presentation by saying "Hello" or "Good morning" helps the audience feel welcome. Then the speaker should catch the audience's attention so they will be interested and curious.

One way to catch the audience's attention is to tell an interesting story related to the ideas in the presentation. When the speaker tells a story, he or she creates a connection to the audience. The audience naturally becomes more involved in the topic, and they want to listen more.

Catch the audience's attention by telling an interesting story at the beginning of your presentation.

Check your comprehension

GO ONLINE

A. Watch a student give a presentation about a new way to advertise. Then answer these two questions.

1. What product is being advertised?

_____

2. What is the new way to advertise the product?

_____

_____

Notice how the speaker catches the audience's attention

GO ONLINE

B. Watch the video again. Think about the information in the strategy box above. List two problems with the way the student caught the audience's attention.

_____

_____

_____

GO ONLINE **C.** The student received some suggestions about his presentation and delivered it again. Watch the new presentation. List two improvements the student made to the way he caught the audience's attention.

_____

_____

_____

PRESENTATION STRATEGY	Strategies for Catching the Audience's Attention through an Interesting Story
	• Tell a story that is partially incomplete so the audience is curious to hear the ideas in your presentation.
	• Tell a story that presents a problem that the ideas in your presentation will solve.
	• Tell a story that shares an experience that your audience can relate to.

List more examples

D. Work with a partner to think of other ways to tell a story that catches the audience's attention. Write your examples here.

_____

_____

_____

Practice catching the audience's attention

E. Stand in front of a group. Tell a story that will begin a presentation in which you describe one aspect of shopping that you like. For example, you could talk about helpful clerks, a beautiful design, or a wide selection of products.

Practice the strategies for catching the audience's attention. Then ask your classmates these two questions:

1. What is one way I effectively caught your attention?

2. What is one way to improve how I catch the audience's attention?

Give a presentation

F. Prepare and deliver a presentation about a product that interests you.

Choose a product that interests you. Describe a new place or a new way to advertise the product. Explain why you believe this advertising campaign would be effective. Show an example.

Use the strategies, and tell the audience a story to catch their attention.

Before you prepare your presentation, review the ideas and vocabulary from this chapter.

A. Work in a group. Imagine that you work in the marketing department of a company that makes backpacks. Your group is in charge of developing a marketing campaign for a new backpack design. The targeted consumers are the students in your school.

Begin by developing a marketing survey. Work with your group to write a list of questions that will help you determine what kinds of ads appeal to the targeted consumers.

Listen and Take Notes

Use the questions to survey students outside of class. Take notes on their answers to the questions, and compile your findings.

Discuss the Results

Using the results of the survey, discuss what type of ads you will use and why. Then plan where to place the ads. Think about where students go, when they go there, and why they go there. Make a list of possible placement areas and give reasons for your choices.

Present Your Plan

Share the results of your survey and your marketing plans with your class. Be sure to catch your audience's attention and to keep your audience's interest by retaining eye contact.

B. Work in a group. Look at two magazines: one for women and one for men. Find an ad for the same type of product, such as skin-care products, in both magazines.

Discuss these Questions

1. What are some of the differences in the ads?

2. How does the ad in the men's magazine appeal to men?

3. How does the ad in the women's magazine appeal to women?

4. If the product is traditionally female, how does the company market it to men? If it is traditionally male, how does the company market it to women?

5. How could the company market this product to people of the opposite gender?

Present Your Findings

Share what you learn with the class. Be sure to also share your ideas on how companies could market to people of the other gender. Give an example or short story to get your audience's attention. Then, keep their attention by using eye contact.

Unit Goals

UNIT

2

Sociology

sociology \ˌsoʊsiˈɑlədʒi\ **The study of human societies and social behavior**

STEP 1 Listen and Apply New Strategies

Think about the topic **A.** Look at the picture. Then discuss the questions below with a partner.

1. How many different things is the woman on the phone doing?

2. Does this image give a true idea about work habits today? Why or why not?

3. Do you think work and life balance is different for women than it is for men? If so, how?

4. Do you think people work more in some countries than in others?

B. Read this article about the choices some people have made to balance work and life.

Life's Labors

At the beginning of the 21st century, many people around the world are better off than they were in the distant past—they are healthier, wealthier, and better educated. When we **analyze** work **trends** around the world, we find that many people work longer hours and have less free time than in the past. Here are the stories of several people's struggles.

Two Aspiring Actors in Los Angeles

Lisa and Harry Robles are trying to find success in the city of dreams. Like many actors, they moved to Los Angeles, California, to pursue film and TV careers. Also like many actors, their income from acting does not meet their needs. To fill the gap, they **juggle** a variety of part-time jobs. This situation is made more difficult by the fact that they are the parents of two young children. Playing the **role** of parent along with their various other roles—in front of the camera and in real life—is tough, but they say it's worth it. They are following their dreams and believe that they will succeed eventually. For now, though, they have little free time. Their daily schedules are busy and complicated, and the whole family has learned to be very **efficient** with time, energy, and money.

A Civil Servant in Seoul

At 39 years of age, Lee is a father of three teens. Unfortunately, he only sees them ten or fifteen minutes each week. He spends most of his life working and commuting to and from his job in Seoul, South Korea. Lee leaves his home at 6:30 a.m. Two hours later, he arrives at his **workplace**. As a civil servant, Lee sits behind a computer for the next twelve hours. He begins his two-hour commute home at 9:00 p.m. Lee feels a lot of **pressure** to perform well. "We always watch what the senior boss thinks of our behavior," he says. When asked about his vacations, Lee says that he takes three days per year. He believes he would lose his job if he took much more.

It turns out that Lee's story is common in South Korea. Working hard is an important **value** in South Korean culture, and the country is known to have the longest working hours in the developed world.

C. With a partner, discuss these questions about the reading.

1. What are some of the things that make Lisa and Harry's life difficult?

2. What are some of the things that make Lee's life difficult?

3. What do all the people in the article have in common?

D. Match the words from the reading with their definitions. Look back at the article on page 29 to check your answers.

_____ **1.** analyze

a. expectations that cause someone to feel worried or nervous

_____ **2.** trend

b. the room or building where people work

_____ **3.** juggle

c. working well, quickly, and without wasting time, energy, or effort

_____ **4.** role

d. to keep two or more activities in progress at the same time

_____ **5.** efficient

e. the function someone has in a particular situation or activity

_____ **6.** workplace

f. belief about what is important in life

_____ **7.** pressure

g. to look closely at a situation in order to try to explain it

_____ **8.** value

h. the way a situation is developing or changing

E. Circle the phrase with a similar meaning to the underlined idiom.

Pedro and Cecilia moved to Florida because they wanted a quieter life, but <u>it turns out</u> that they are busier now than they were in New York.

a. it is changing   **b.** it is true   **c.** it is nice

F. Discuss these questions in a group. Share your answers with the class.

1. The stories in the reading show examples of the growing trend toward working longer hours. Is this trend true for people you know? Give examples to support your opinion.

2. The people in the reading seem to enjoy their lives even though they feel a lot of pressure. Do you think that most people enjoy their work?

G. With a partner, discuss three things that you have learned from the reading and from your discussion about work trends.

1. _____

2. _____

3. _____

H. To help you understand the listening strategy, discuss the situation below with a partner, and answer the question.

You are in a large university classroom listening to a two-hour lecture. The professor talks about one idea and then quickly moves to another idea. This happens over and over again. What might be difficult about this situation?

LISTENING STRATEGY

Recognize Lecture Language for Transitions

Professors use a variety of expressions throughout a lecture to signal a new idea or the end of one idea and the beginning of a new idea. Think of these transitions as road signs that help you find your way.

Listen for transitions—the expressions that help you follow the flow of ideas in a lecture.

Expressions That Signal a New Idea
- Let me start with . . .
- Next, let's talk about . . .
- I want to focus on . . .
- Now . . .
- First, let's look at . . .
- What I want to discuss now is . . .

Expressions That Signal the End of One Idea and the Beginning of a New Idea
- Now that we have talked about . . . let's talk about . . .
- Let's move on to . . .
- That's enough about . . . Let's go to the next point.

List more examples

I. Work with a partner to think of other expressions that signal a transition. Write your examples here.

_____

_____

_____

Recognize transition lecture language

J. Read the excerpt from a lecture about work habits. Then underline the lecture language that signals a transition

Marriage and work is an interesting topic, so let me start with the point that married couples have reacted in a variety of ways to the pressures they feel when both the husband and wife work. We've seen that it's a struggle for some couples, and somehow other couples can make it work. Let's move on to some of the polling data I collected with my colleagues last summer so that we can discover some of the reasons for these reactions.

K. Listen to the practice lecture about the work lives of three family members. Match the name of each person to the description of her work experience.

___ **1.** Dina   **a.** She has never worked.

___ **2.** Laura   **b.** She has worked in a fast food restaurant and in an office.

___ **3.** Maria   **c.** She works in a law firm.

L. Listen to the practice lecture again. Write down the lecture language that signals a transition from one idea to another. Then listen again, and write down the idea that follows the transition.

1. Transition lecture language: _____

_____

New idea: _____

_____

2. Transition lecture language: _____

_____

New idea: _____

_____

3. Transition lecture language: _____

_____

New idea: _____

_____

4. Transition lecture language: _____

_____

New idea: _____

_____

NOTE-TAKING STRATEGY

Use Symbols to Represent Words and Ideas

The average professor speaks at a rate of about 125 words a minute—too fast to write down every word. Using symbols will help you keep up with the professor's lecture. Use symbols in place of full words and phrases to write down ideas more quickly.

Commonly Used Symbols

=	equals, is the same	#	number
≠	is not the same	w/	with
>	is more than	w/out	without
<	is less than	+	and
♂	man	↓	to go down, decrease, lower
♀	woman	↑	to go up, increase, higher
△	change	!	(to mark importance)

List more examples

A. Work with a partner to think of other symbols that represent words and ideas. Write your examples here.

_____   _____

_____   _____

_____   _____

Use symbols

B. Read these sentences from a lecture on work habits. Take notes using symbols to represent words and ideas.

1. It is important to know that the number of Internet businesses is increasing every day

 # Internet businesses ↑ every day—!

2. One major change is that business today is international—it's not the same as it was 30 years ago.

_____

3. Many men and women are employed and taking care of children.

_____

4. Companies try to stay competitive in two ways: They try to have lower costs than other companies, and they try to maximize production so that they can make more money.

_____

_____

C. Before the lecture, think about everything you have learned and discussed on the topic of work habits in the 21st century. What do you expect to learn from the lecture? Write three predictions below. Compare your predictions with a partner.

1. _____

2. _____

3. _____

D. Watch the lecture, and take notes using symbols to represent words and ideas. Remember to listen for the lecture language that signals a transition.

Topic:

Research on how U.S. people work

Reasons people feel busy

In the workplace

Additional point

E. Check the statement that best describes how well you were able to recognize the lecture language. Explain your answer.

I was able to recognize the change from one idea to another ___.

a. all of the time   **b.** most of the time   **c.** sometimes   **d.** not often

F. Use your notes to answer these questions.

1. What did the researchers learn about the amount of work that people feel they are doing?

_____

_____

_____

2. What are the three reasons for the increased feeling of busyness among working people today?

_____

_____

_____

3. What is the big change in the workplace that is causing workers to feel busier?

_____

_____

_____

4. Although people are busier, they like their jobs. Why is this true?

_____

_____

_____

G. Were you able to answer the questions in Exercise F using the information in your notes? Compare and discuss your notes with a few other students. Help each other fill in any missing information. Revise your notes.

H. Work with a partner, and take turns. Review your notes from the lecture. Then summarize the main points of the lecture for your partner. Talk for 2–3 minutes only.

ACADEMIC DISCUSSION STRATEGY

Interrupt and Ask for Clarification

It is normal to not understand everything you hear during a discussion. In most classrooms, students are expected to take responsibility when they don't understand what the professor or a classmate says. During a discussion, politely interrupt, and ask questions when you don't understand.

Non-Verbal Ways to Interrupt
- Make eye contact with the speaker.
- Make a small hand gesture.
- Raise your hand.

Phrases for Interrupting
- Excuse me, . . .
- I'm sorry, . . .
- Before we go on, . . .

Questions to Ask When You Don't Understand
- Could you repeat that?
- Could you say that again please?
- Could you explain that?
- What does . . . mean?

List more examples

A. Work with a partner to think of other ways to interrupt and ask for clarification. Write your examples here.

_____

_____

Practice interrupting and asking for clarification

B. In a group, read and discuss the questions below. Keep the conversation going until every student has had a chance to practice interrupting and asking for clarification. Use your own ideas or the ones given below.

1. What kind of work have you done? Where?

   Possible ideas

office work	in a bank	part-time / full-time
in a bookstore	in a restaurant	in a convenience store
babysitting	in a business	repair work

2. What kinds of technology do you (or will you) use at your job?

   Possible ideas

   | computers | cell phones | scanners |
   | cash registers | digital photography | health-care equipment |

Discuss the ideas in the lecture

C. Discuss these ideas with your classmates. Remember to use the phrases for interrupting and asking for clarification.

1. One trend described in the lecture is that people feel busier because they have to juggle many responsibilities. Is this true for you?

2. The lecture describes people in the U.S. as being very busy when they work. In your opinion, what are some of the positive effects of this, and what are some of the negative effects?

3. According to the lecture, new technological developments have made it necessary for workers to "think and talk" at the same time. Is this true for you? Would you like to work this way? Why or why not?

4. Look back at your notes. What was another idea in the lecture that you found important or interesting? Tell the class why you think it is important or interesting, and ask for your classmates' opinions.

STEP 4 **Present Your Knowledge**

PRESENTATION STRATEGY

Create Rapport with the Audience Throughout a Presentation

It is important for a speaker to create rapport—that is, a friendly relationship—with the audience throughout a presentation. When the speaker makes a connection with the audience, by mentioning what they all have in common, the audience becomes more comfortable with the speaker. A comfortable audience is more likely to pay attention to what the speaker is saying. A speaker can create rapport by using effective eye contact, smiling, and asking the audience if they understand.

Create rapport with your audience to help them feel comfortable and enjoy listening.

Check your comprehension

GO ONLINE

A. Watch a student give a presentation about typical work habits in one country. Then answer these two questions.

1. What is the name of the country?

_____

2. What are three industries in the country?

_____

_____

Notice how the speaker creates rapport

GO ONLINE

B. Watch the video again. Think about the information in the strategy box above. List two problems with the student's rapport with the audience.

_____

_____

_____

GO ONLINE **C.** The student received some suggestions about his presentation and delivered it again. Watch the new presentation. List two improvements the student made to successfully create rapport with the audience throughout the presentation.

_____

_____

_____

Strategies for Creating Rapport with Your Audience

Smile and make eye contact with everyone in the audience.

Point out that you have something in common with the audience, such as an experience, habit, or understanding. Use expressions like the following.
- All of us have seen . . .
- If you're like me, you . . .
- We all like to . . .

From time to time during your presentation, check to be sure the audience understands your ideas. Use questions like the following.
- Is that clear to everyone?
- Does everyone understand this point?

List more examples

D. Work with a partner to think of other ways to create rapport. Write your examples in your notebook.

Practice creating rapport

E. Stand in front of a group of classmates. Tell your audience about the job of someone you know—a friend or relative. Give the job title, and explain what the person does at the job. Practice the strategies for creating effective rapport with your audience.

After you finish, have your classmates give you feedback on your rapport with the audience. Ask them these two questions:

1. What are two ways I effectively created rapport with the audience?

2. What is one way to improve my rapport with the audience?

Give a presentation

F. Prepare and deliver a presentation about work habits.

Choose a country, and do research to find out about the work habits of people in that country. Briefly tell about the country. Include information about the major industries, the average work schedule, and the percentage of people working at home versus in a workplace.

Give your opinion about whether you think you would be satisfied to work in that country. Explain the reasons for your opinion. Use the strategies for creating rapport with your audience.

Before you prepare your presentation, review the ideas and vocabulary from this chapter.

Think about the topic **A.** Read these graphs about leisure time activities in the United States. Then work with a partner to discuss the questions below.

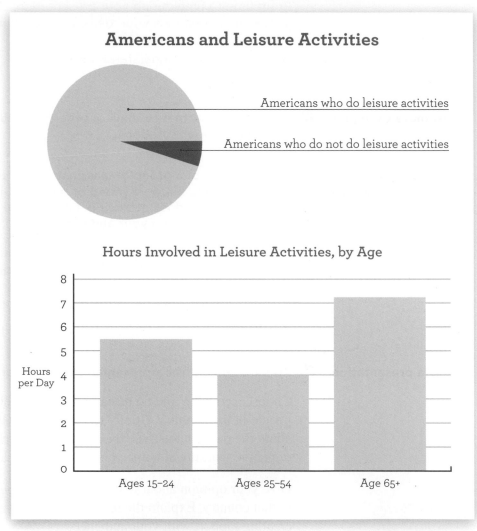

Americans and Leisure Activities

Americans who do leisure activities

Americans who do not do leisure activities

Hours Involved in Leisure Activities, by Age

Hours per Day

| | Ages 15–24 | Ages 25–54 | Age 65+ |

1. Why does the amount of time spent on leisure vary with age?

2. For each age range, is this enough leisure time or too much? Why?

3. Do you think the finding in the chart is about right for your age group? How much time do you spend on leisure activities each day?

B. Read this article about trends in the way Americans spend their leisure time.

All or Nothing: Current Trends in Leisure Time

Every year since 1995, the Harris Poll, a **survey** group, has asked Americans, average age 25, to name their two or three favorite leisure time activities. The survey's goal is to identify trends in favorite leisure activities over time.

The information gathered in the Harris survey shows the types of activities that people do in their leisure time. It does not, however, show the ways in which they do them. These stories of individuals show two different trends.

Multitask: The "All" Approach

Jean Flores represents the trend toward multitasking. She works sixty hours a week and cares for her husband and parents. She lives her life at a fast **pace** and doesn't have much time for herself. Her leisure time is at six o'clock in the morning. Exercising is Flores' method of **relaxation**. Working out at her gym on an exercise bicycle helps her stay healthy and avoid getting **stressed out**. While she is exercising, however, Flores also likes to read her email and listen to the news on the radio. Flores wants to get the most value from her leisure time, so she **multitasks** as much as possible. She feels that multitasking gives her the relaxation she needs but also prepares her for her day.

No-Brainer: The "Nothing" Approach

Like Jean Flores, Sam Bronsky also has almost no time for himself. He works three jobs and rarely has a day off. When he does manage to get a little free time, he wants to escape from his **exhausting** schedule and get out of the city. He likes to **hang out** on the beach with friends or go fishing. When he is not able to go away, he enjoys gardening in his backyard. Sam calls his leisure time preferences **no-brainer** activities. They allow him to recover from his stressful work schedule and relax, but they do not require him to think about work or daily life.

For most people, these two approaches overlap. Some people multitask in the evenings and do no-brainer activities on weekends. Think of leisure time as a line, with *multitasking* at one end and *no-brainer* at the other end. Where do you stand?

FAVORITE LEISURE ACTIVITIES	
Reading	29%
Watching TV	18%
Spending Time with Family	14%
Computer Activities	9%
Going to Movies	7%
Fishing	7%
Gardening	6%

C. With a partner, discuss these questions about the reading.

1. How does Jean Flores spend her leisure time?

2. How does Sam Bronsky spend his leisure time?

D. Circle the answer that correctly completes the definition of the underlined word. Look back at the article on page 41 to check your answers.

1. A <u>survey</u> is a set of questions that helps researchers _____ people's opinions or behavior.

   a. find out about   **b.** form

2. <u>Pace</u> is the _____ at which something happens or is done.

   a. direction   **b.** speed

3. <u>Relaxation</u> is a way of feeling calm and _____ yourself.

   a. bored with   **b.** enjoying

4. To feel <u>stressed-out</u> means you are so _____ that you cannot relax.

   a. worried and tired   **b.** happy and tired

5. <u>Multitasking</u> means doing _____ at a time.

   a. only one thing   **b.** more than one thing

6. Something that is <u>exhausting</u> makes you feel _____ tired.

   a. extremely   **b.** a little

7. A <u>no-brainer</u> activity is something that needs _____ thought.

   a. very little   **b.** a lot of

E. Circle the phrase with a similar meaning to the underlined idiom.

After the kids leave for school, Chris Flores likes to <u>hang out</u> for a while and have a cup of tea before she starts her busy day.

   a. do household chores   **b.** not do very much

F. Discuss these questions in a group. Share your answers with the class.

1. Do you think the results of the Harris survey are generally true for the people you know? If the Harris Poll did this survey in your school, what other activities might appear on the list?

2. In your personal leisure time, are you more like Jean or Sam?

G. With a partner, discuss three things that you have learned from the reading and from your discussion about leisure time.

H. To help you understand the listening strategy, discuss the situation below with a partner, and answer the question.

Experts estimate that students learn up to 1,000 new words per year from reading and lectures. How can a student prepare for receiving new words during a lecture?

LISTENING STRATEGY

Recognize Lecture Language That Signals a Definition

Professors often use new words as they explain new information or ideas. They also use a variety of expressions to present definitions for those words. Listen for the words and expressions that professors use to signal a definition.

Expressions That Signal a Definition

- that is, . . .
- in other words, . . .
- X, meaning . . .
- by X, I mean . . .
- X means . . .
- What I mean by X is . . .

Another common signal for a definition is a rhetorical question. Rhetorical questions are given for the purpose of preparing the listener for the answer. They are not questions that the professor wants students to answer:

- What do I mean by X? Well, I mean . . .
- What is X? X is . . .

List more examples **I.** Work with a partner to think of other expressions that signal a definition. Write your examples in your notebook.

Recognize definition lecture language **J.** Read the excerpt from a lecture about leisure activities. Underline and label the phrases to be defined, the lecture language that signals the definitions, and the definitions.

People who take the no-brainer approach to leisure time like to spend time on things that are a piece of cake, that is, things that are not too challenging. These kinds of activities, like watching TV and fishing, allow people to spend time in a restful way.

People who multitask spend their time doing many things at once. They think that this is an efficient way to spend the little free time that they have. These people really do not like to fritter away their time. What I mean by fritter away their time is waste their time. The idea of wasting time is not a relaxing concept for them.

In fact, one of the things we notice about multitaskers is that they are very thrifty, . . . thrifty in how they use their time. By thrifty, I mean that they use their time carefully without wasting it.

K. Listen to a practice lecture about how four different people spend their leisure time. Match the name of each person to the type of leisure activity he or she enjoys.

___ **1.** Lily   **a.** nothing

___ **2.** Marvin   **b.** skateboarding

___ **3.** Taka   **c.** playing and watching soccer

___ **4.** Jo   **d.** bungee-jumping

L. Listen to the practice lecture again. Write down the lecture language that signals a definition. Then listen again, and write down the definition.

1. Word: findings

Lecture language: _____

Definition: _____

_____

2. Word: charisma

Lecture language: _____

Definition: _____

_____

3. Word: bungee jumping

Lecture language: _____

Definition: _____

_____

4. Word: fakie

Lecture language: _____

Definition: _____

_____

5. Word: zilch

Lecture language: _____

Definition: _____

_____

NOTE-TAKING STRATEGY

Use Abbreviations to Represent Longer Words

An abbreviation is a shortened form of a word. Using abbreviations along with symbols will help you keep up with the professor's lecture. Use abbreviations in place of full words to write down ideas more quickly.

Commonly Used Abbreviations

adv	advantage	e.g.	example	info	information
avg	average	est	estimate	max	maximum
aprox	approximately	esp	especially	min	minimum
btwn	between	etc.	etcetera	pg	page
cont	continued	i.d.	identity	pop	population
diff	difference, different	i.e.	in other words	vs.	versus
ea	each	imp	important		

List more examples

A. Work with a partner to think of other abbreviations you can use when writing notes. Write your examples here.

_____   _____   _____

_____   _____   _____

Use abbreviations

B. Read these sentences from a lecture on leisure. Take notes using abbreviations to represent words and ideas.

1. Each year the Harris Poll conducts a survey of Americans. For each survey that they conduct, they focus on different parts of the population.

   Harris Poll ea yr conducts survey of Ams. ea survey focuses

   on diff pop

2. This leisure survey focused on people with the average age of 25. All of the surveys help them identify important trends.

   _____

   _____

3. Experts research how the American population spends leisure time versus how they spend their work time.

   _____

   _____

Make predictions

See page 8

C. Before the lecture, think about everything you have learned and discusssed on the topic of leisure time. What do you expect to learn from the lecture? Write three predictions below. Compare your predictions with a partner.

1. _____

2. _____

3. _____

Watch the lecture

GO ONLINE

D. Watch the lecture, and take notes using abbreviations and symbols. Remember to listen for the lecture language that signals a definition.

Topic:

How people spend their time at work

First way people organize their leisure time

First example

Second example

Second way that people organize their leisure time

Reasons

E. Check the statement that best describes how well you were able to recognize the lecture language.

I was able to recognize the lecture language for definitions ____.

a. all of the time   **b.** most of the time   **c.** sometimes   **d.** not often

F. Use your notes to answer these questions.

1. What are two reactions that people have to the increased feeling of busyness?

_____

_____

_____

2. What is one example of how people multitask during leisure time?

_____

_____

_____

3. What is one example of a no-brainer leisure activity?

_____

_____

_____

4. Why do some people become couch potatoes?

_____

_____

_____

G. Were you able to answer the questions in Exercise F using the information in your notes? Compare your notes with a few other students. Help each other fill in any missing information. Revise your notes.

H. Work with a partner, and take turns. Review your notes from the lecture. Then summarize the main points of the lecture for your partner. Talk for 2–3 minutes only.

ACADEMIC DISCUSSION STRATEGY

Ask for More Information

During a discussion, you might be interested in an idea and want to understand it better, or you might need to know more about it for a test or an assignment. In a discussion, politely ask questions to get more information about a point or idea.

Expressions for Asking for More Information

- Could you explain more about . . .?
- Could you tell me more about . . .?
- Give me an example of . . .?
- Could you explain that in more detail?
- What's the difference between . . . and . . .?
- How does that work?
- What do you mean by that?
- What's an example of that?

List more examples

A. Work with a partner to think of other ways to ask for more information during a discussion. Write your examples here.

_____

_____

_____

Practice asking for more information

B. In a group, read and discuss the questions below. Keep the conversation going until every student has had a chance to practice asking for more information. Use your own ideas or the ones given below.

1. What do you and your friends do in your leisure time?

   Possible ideas

play sports	read	drive around or hang out
watch TV	shop	listen to music

2. What are some of the differences between reading and watching TV?

   Possible ideas

Reading	**Watching TV**
quiet	lively
have to use your imagination	a lot of choice
nice for spending time alone	feels social

Discuss the ideas in the lecture

C. Discuss these ideas with your classmates. Remember to use the phrases for asking for more information.

1. Do people in other cultures spend their leisure time in similar ways to people in the United States or very differently? Explain your answer.

2. The lecture describes Americans as busy when they do leisure activities. In your opinion, what are some of the positive effects of this, and what are some of the negative effects?

3. The lecture says that some people react to a busy work life by being couch potatoes in their leisure time. In your opinion, what are some of the positive effects of this, and what are some of the negative effects?

4. Look back at your notes. What was another idea in the lecture that you found important or interesting? Tell the class why you think it is important or interesting, and ask for your classmates' opinions.

PRESENTATION STRATEGY

Signal a Transition Between Speakers

It is common for a group of speakers to give a presentation together. Each member of the group gives a different part of the presentation. It's important for a speaker to introduce the next speaker and the topic of the next part before the new speaker begins. Signaling these transitions between speakers helps the audience follow the flow of information.

Use transitions between speakers to help the audience follow the flow of information in a group presentation.

Check your comprehension

A. Watch a group of students give a presentation about leisure habits. Then answer these two questions.

1. What leisure activity did they survey?

_____

2. What are two interesting things they learned from the survey?

_____

_____

Notice transitions between speakers

B. Watch the video again. Think about the information in the strategy box above. List two problems with the way each speaker transitions to another speaker.

_____

_____

_____

 C. The students received some suggestions about their presentation and delivered it again. Watch the new presentation. List two improvements the students made to the way they signaled a transition between speakers.

_____

_____

_____

Expressions for Signaling Transitions Between Speakers
- Now, Marta will talk about . . .
- Now I'd like to turn it over to Kang who will tell you about . . .
- At this point, Habiba will present . . .

List more examples

D. Work with a partner to think of other ways to signal a transition between speakers. Write your examples in your notebook.

Practice effectively signaling a transition between speakers

E. Work with a group to prepare and give a very short presentation on the leisure activities of the whole group. Answer the following questions.

- What are the favorite leisure activities of the group members?

- What are the least favorite leisure activities of the group members?

- What are some leisure activities the group wants to try?

Have each student talk about the answer to one of these questions. Practice the strategies for signaling a transition between speakers. The first speaker should conclude the presentation so that everyone has a chance to transition to another speaker.

After you finish, have your classmates give you feedback on your transitions between speakers. Ask them these two questions:

1. What are two ways we effectively signaled a transition between speakers?

2. What is one way to improve our transitions between speakers?

Give a presentation

F. Prepare and deliver a group presentation about how your classmates spend their leisure time.

Choose one of the following leisure activities:

- Watching TV
- Using the Internet
- Socializing with friends
- Reading
- Listening to music
- Playing video games
- Playing sports

Create survey questions to find out how much time each of your classmates spends doing the leisure activity.

Present the results of your survey to the class. Include the questions you asked, the results of the survey, and any insights you drew from the results. Use the strategies for signaling a transition between speakers.

Before you prepare your presentation, review the ideas and vocabulary from this chapter.

A. Work in a group. Assign each person a different age group to survey: 13–17, 18–22, 23–30, 31–40, over 40.

Survey these age groups outside of class using the survey questions below.

1. What do you usually do in your leisure time?

2. How much time do you spend on leisure activities in a week?

3. How much money do you usually spend each week or month on leisure activities?

Discuss the Results

Discuss the results of your survey. Draw three to five general conclusions based on your findings.

Present Your Conclusions

Share your results and conclusions with the class. Then compare your conclusions with other groups.

B. Discuss the following information about leisure in the workplace.

Some companies make leisure activities available to employees in the workplace. They provide tennis courts, swimming pools, fitness equipment, pool tables, and outdoor parks for employee use. Some give employees a day off to go to an amusement park together.

As a class, discuss the pros and cons of providing such activities in the workplace. Then divide into two groups. One group will prepare to present the benefits of the approach. The second group will present the drawbacks.

Present Your Side

Debate the pros and cons of providing workplace leisure activities. Signal a transition between speakers both within your own group and between your group and the opposing group.

C. Research changes in workplace technology.

Listen and Take Notes

Interview working people who are at least 50 years old. Find out what types of technology they used prior to 1980 and what technology they have used since 1980. How have changes in technology affected their work and their lives? Take notes of their answers to your questions.

Present Your Findings

Share the results of your interviews with the class. Explain how technology has changed lives since the 1980s.

Unit Goals

CHAPTER 5
Learn some of the reasons behind food choice

Listening Strategy
• Recognize lecture language that signals an example

Note-Taking Strategy
• Organize key material into a visual form

Academic Discussion Strategy
• Agree and disagree with others in the discussion

Presentation Strategy
• Conclude a presentation by summarizing the main points

CHAPTER 6
Learn about some unique solutions to pollution

Listening Strategy
• Recognize lecture language that signals an explanation

Note-Taking Strategy
• Describe the visuals used in a lecture

Academic Discussion Strategy
• Support your opinions in the discussion

Presentation Strategy
• Open the floor to questions from your audience

UNIT
3

Science

science \ˈsaɪəns\ The study of and knowledge about the physical world and natural laws

CHAPTER 5 Science and Pleasure: What We Eat

Think about the topic   **A.** Look at the cartoon. Then discuss the questions below with a partner.

"I'm going to order a broiled skinless chicken breast, but I want you to bring me lasagna and garlic bread by mistake."

1. What are some of the differences between the food the woman is going to order and the food that she really wants to eat?

2. Why do you think that she chooses one but hopes to eat the other?

Read to build background knowledge

See page 2

B. Read this article about government recommendations for nutrition.

The Food Guide Pyramid

Many governments have agencies that make **recommendations** to help citizens maintain healthy **diets**. They first consider the **nutrition** that the human body needs for energy and growth—vitamins, proteins, and minerals. They use this information as the **source** for their recommendations. These agencies inform people of what food they should eat to meet their nutritional requirements. The governments hope that the recommendations will have a positive **influence** on what people eat.

In 1992, the U.S. Department of Agriculture (USDA) created the Food Guide Pyramid to share their recommendations with people. The pyramid was a simple diagram representing many pages of recommendations. In 2005, diet was considered a serious issue in the United States because 65 percent of adults ages 20 to 74 were overweight. The USDA updated the pyramid so that each person could get more personalized advice about diet and exercise. There were 12 versions of the diagram, depending on a person's activity level and need for calories.

A number of governments use food pyramids, including the Philippines and Poland. The UK and Mexico have a plate design for their nutrition guidelines. Some countries have more creative designs like

China's Food Pagoda

China's Food Pagoda. All of these diagrams are similar in terms of the food groups they include: grains, fruits and vegetables, and proteins (meat, beans). Most also include dairy (milk) products and vegetable oils. The agencies also encourage drinking water and exercising. Many discourage eating fatty and sugary foods.

There was some **controversy** about the recommendations on the 2005 USDA pyramid. Some people thought it should say more about the foods to avoid, not just the foods to choose. Others were happy to see that the recommended serving sizes were more specific. The **debate** continued as scientists, researchers, and the public voiced their opinions. Then in 2011, the U.S. government introduced a new plate design, similar to ones used in Mexico and the UK. However, many Americans are still more familiar with the pyramid.

Although there may be controversy and a variety of designs, people should not use these as reasons to ignore the recommendations. True, it might be hard to follow them sometimes, but people should not **give up** on their health. The goal of all nutrition diagrams is to encourage people not to eat only for **pleasure**, but to think about how to get the nutrients and exercise their bodies need.

U.S. Food Guide Pyramid

C. With a partner, discuss these questions about the reading.

1. What is the purpose of food guide diagrams?

2. What was one controversy about the recommendations in the USDA's 2005 revised food pyramid?

3. What is one thing that all food guide diagrams include?

D. Match the words from the reading with their definitions. Look back at the article on page 55 to check your answers.

____ 1. recommendation   **a.** the right type of food for good health

____ 2. diet   **b.** where something starts or comes from

____ 3. nutrition   **c.** a discussion in which people take opposite sides

____ 4. source   **d.** the food that a person usually eats

____ 5. influence   **e.** the feeling of being happy or satisfied

____ 6. controversy   **f.** a statement about what should be done

____ 7. debate   **g.** an effect on someone's behavior

____ 8. pleasure   **h.** public disagreement about something

E. Circle the answer with a similar meaning to the underlined idiom.

Following the USDA recommendations can be confusing, but people should not <u>give up</u> and ignore the recommendations completely.

a. stop trying   **b.** ask questions   **c.** argue

F. Discuss these questions in a group. Share your answers with the class.

1. In what situations would you consider recommendations from experts about the food you eat? Describe the situations.

2. Are there times when you don't think about your diet at all and just eat whatever you want? When? Why?

G. With a partner, discuss three things that you have learned from the reading and from your discussion about nutrition and the food pyramid.

1. _____

2. _____

3. _____

H. To help you understand the listening strategy, discuss the situation below with a partner, and answer the question.

Imagine someone asks you, "What is a carbohydrate?" Without using a dictionary, what is a quick and easy way to communicate the meaning?

Recognize Lecture Language for Examples

Professors use examples throughout their lectures. These examples of specific things help students understand general ideas.

Listen for the words and expressions that professors use to signal an example.

Expressions That Signal an Example

For Actual Examples
- For example, . . .
- Take . . . , for example.
- Here is a perfect example of . . .
- Here are some examples of . . .
- To illustrate, let's look at . . .
- For instance, . . .
- Such as . . .
- Like . . .

For Hypothetical (Unreal) Examples
- Let's say . . .
- Take something like . . .

I. Work with a partner to think of other expressions that signal an actual or hypothetical example. Write your examples here.

_____

_____

J. Read this excerpt from a lecture on the Food Guide Pyramid. Underline and label the lecture language that signals an example and the examples.

On a recent food pyramid, we saw something new. Each person could get personalized recommendations about diet and exercise. Let's look at what they recommended. For moderate exercise, here are some examples of the kind of physical activity that was recommended: walking quickly (about 3 1/2 miles per hour), hiking, gardening or yard work, golf, or bicycling.

But, some physical activities are not intense enough to help you meet the recommendations. They are activities like these — the walking that you do while grocery shopping, and doing light household chores. Although you are moving, these activities do not increase your heart rate.

K. Listen to an excerpt from a lecture on the Food Guide Pyramid. Match the terms that the professor uses with the examples.

____ **1.** orange band   **a.** vegetables

____ **2.** green band   **b.** fruit

____ **3.** red band   **c.** grains

____ **4.** yellow band   **d.** oils/fats

L. Listen to the excerpt again. Write down the lecture language that signals an example. Then listen again, and write down the examples.

1. Idea: grains

Example lecture language: _____

Example: _____

2. Idea: vegetables

Example lecture language: _____

Example: _____

3. Idea: fruit

Example lecture language: _____

Example: _____

4. Idea: oils/fats

Example lecture language: _____

Example: _____

5. Idea: milk

Example lecture language: _____

Example: _____

6. Idea: meat and beans

Example lecture language: _____

Example: _____

NOTE-TAKING
STRATEGY

Use a Visual Form

Sometimes it is easier to record and remember an idea when you represent it as a picture or some sort of graphic image. In your notes, record information in a visual form to remind yourself how the points relate to each other.

To represent a progression or process, put the key idea in the center at the top of the page. Then put points and examples into columns and connect them with arrows (← ↓ ↑ →) and plus signs (+) to show relationships.

The process of digestion involves many of the body's organs, such as the stomach, intestines, liver, and kidneys. Digestion begins in the mouth. We chew and swallow. Swallowed food is then pushed into the esophagus through the throat, which is between the mouth and the esophagus. The food enters the stomach from the esophagus. The stomach has three things to do. First, the stomach must store the swallowed food and liquid. Then it mixes the food and liquid with digestive juices. The stomach's final task is to empty its contents into the small intestine.

Organs for Digestion
(stomach, intestines, liver, kidneys)
Mouth
– chew + swallow then push
↓
throat
+
esophagus
↓
stomach
does 3 things

store	→	mix	→	empty
food		w/ digest		into small
		juices		intestine

Analyze the notes   **A.** In your notebook, answer these questions about the lecture excerpt and notes above.

1. What was the main point of the lecture? How do you know?

2. How does the student represent examples?

3. How do you know the order of the steps?

4. How does the student show that the stomach has three tasks?

B. Read this excerpt from a lecture on digestion. Take notes in your notebook using a visual form.

> **Digestion involves three processes. These are, first, the mixing of food; second, the movement of food through the digestive tract; and third, the chemical breakdown of the large molecules of food into smaller molecules. Digestion begins in the mouth, when we chew and swallow, and is completed in the small intestine.**

C. Before the lecture, think about everything you have learned and discussed on the topic of nutrition and eating. What do you expect to learn from the lecture? Write three predictions in your notebook. Compare your predictions with a partner.

D. Watch the lecture, and take notes, using a visual form if helpful. Remember to listen for the lecture language that signals an example.

Two basic purposes of food

Reasons people don't take USDA advice

Differences between French and American attitudes toward food

French approach to food

American approach to food

E. Check the statement that best describes how well you were able to recognize the lecture language.

I was able to recognize when the professor gave examples ___.

a. all of the time   **b.** most of the time   **c.** sometimes   **d.** not often

F. Use your notes to answer these questions.

1. What are the two basic purposes of food?

    _____

    _____

    _____

2. Why don't people always take the recommendations of the USDA dietary guidelines?

    _____

    _____

    _____

3. What did the specific example of potato chips tell you about nutritional information in general?

    _____

    _____

    _____

4. Name at least three of the differences between the French attitude toward food and the American attitude toward food?

    _____

    _____

    _____

G. Were you able to answer the questions in Exercise F using the information in your notes? Compare and discuss your notes with a few other students. Help each other fill in any missing information. Revise your notes.

H. Work with a partner, and take turns. Review your notes from the lecture. Then summarize the main points of the lecture for your partner. Talk for 2–3 minutes only.

ACADEMIC DISCUSSION STRATEGY

Agree and Disagree

During a group discussion, you might want to agree with another student and build on his or her point or disagree with another student and explain why. This type of exchange is good because it indicates how well you understand the topic. When you disagree, it's important to show respect for the opinions of others. When you show respect for others, everyone is more likely to stay involved in the discussion. Use expressions to agree or disagree with others in a discussion.

Expressions for Agreeing and Disagreeing

Agreeing	**Disagreeing**
• I agree with John. . . .	• I'm afraid I don't agree. . . .
• That's a good point. . . .	• I'm sorry, but I have to disagree. . . .
• I agree with Maria's point. . . .	• I disagree with Isabel. . . .
• S/he's right. . . .	• No, I don't think that's true. . . .
• I think Josue has the right idea. . . .	• I see your point, but . . .

List more examples

A. Work with a partner to think of other expressions you can use to agree or disagree with an idea in a discussion. Write your examples here.

_____

_____

_____

Practice agreeing and disagreeing

B. In a group, read and discuss the questions below. Keep the conversation going until every student has had a chance to practice using the language for agreeing and disagreeing. Use your own ideas or the ones given below.

1. Do you think it is necessary to eat breakfast in the morning?

Possible Ideas

Necessary:	**Not Necessary**
gives you energy	makes you sleepy
keeps you feeling full	wastes time
helps you concentrate	too sugary

2. Is American food healthy or unhealthy?

Possible Ideas

Healthy:	**Unhealthy**
lots of fresh vegetables	big portions
organic food	lots of high fat food
low-salt choices	fast food

Discuss the ideas in the lecture

C. Discuss these ideas with your classmates. Remember to use the phrases for agreeing and disagreeing.

1. Do you think it is more important to consider nutritional needs or pleasure when choosing food? Why?

2. Where do you get information about the health quality of food? Do you ever find this information confusing? Why?

3. The professor wraps up the lecture by saying that how we eat and how we feel about eating is just as important as what we eat. Explain what you think the professor means. Do you agree or disagree with this opinion? Why?

PRESENTATION
STRATEGY

Conclude Your Presentation by Summarizing the Main Points

The end of a presentation gives the speaker an opportunity to remind the audience of the speaker's most important points. The audience has listened to many ideas throughout the presentation, so the conclusion allows the speaker to stress the ideas that he or she wants the audience to remember. One effective way to do this is to summarize the main points of the presentation.

Conclude your presentation by briefly summarizing your most important points.

Check your comprehension

GO ONLINE

A. Watch a student give a presentation about food. Then answer these two questions.

1. What is the name of the dish?

_____

2. What is the student's opinion about the dish?

_____

_____

Notice how the speaker concludes the presentation

GO ONLINE

B. Watch the video again. Think about the information in the strategy box above. List two problems with the way the speaker concluded her presentation.

_____

_____

_____

GO ONLINE

C. The student received some suggestions about the presentation and delivered it again. Watch the new presentation. List two improvements the student made to her conclusion.

_____

_____

_____

_____

Expressions for Signaling a Concluding Summary
- I tried to show you that . . .
- As we've seen today, . . .
- To sum up, . . .

List more examples

D. Work with a partner to think of other ways to signal a concluding summary. Write your examples here.

_____

_____

_____

Practice summarizing the main points in your conclusion

E. Work in a group. Stand in front of your group. Describe what you usually eat for breakfast, lunch, and dinner.

Give important details, but don't give every detail about what you eat. Conclude your presentation with a summary. Practice the strategies for concluding a presentation by summarizing the main points.

After you finish, ask your classmates these two questions:

1. In what way did I successfully summarize the most important points in my conclusion?

2. What is one way to improve how I summarize the most important points in my conclusion?

Give a presentation

F. Prepare and deliver a presentation about a food that is popular in your country.

Address each of the following ideas in your presentation:

- Introduce the food—what is it called, and what does it consist of?
- Explain when and where people usually eat this food.
- Describe the main nutrients in the food.
- Give your opinion about whether the food is healthy or not. Use dietary guidelines from your country or region to support your opinion.

Use the strategies for concluding a presentation by summarizing the most important points.

Before you prepare your presentation, review the ideas and vocabulary from this chapter.

STEP 1 Listen and Apply New Strategies

Think about the topic   **A.** Look at the picture. Then discuss the questions below with a partner.

1. What are some forms of pollution? Does every urban area have every form? Why or why not?

2. Are factories or individuals more responsible for pollution?

3. How can governments prevent or reduce pollution?

4. What can you do to prevent or reduce pollution?

B. Read this article about how children's health issues have inspired new pollution laws.

The Effects of Air Pollution on Children

The average adult breathes over 3,000 gallons of air every day. When you compare body weight and the size of their lungs, children breathe even more. It is not surprising, then, that air pollution has a bigger negative **impact** on the children in any **population** than on the adults. Air pollution can cause breathing problems, disorders in the nervous system, and an increased risk of cancer.

The American Lung Association **paints a picture** of why children are so affected by air pollution. Children are generally more active than adults. As a result, they breathe more rapidly and take more pollution deep into their lungs. Children also often breathe through their mouths, not through their noses. The mouth cannot filter out pollutants as well as the nose. Finally, children generally spend an average of 50 percent more time outdoors than adults do, especially during summer months. Air pollution levels are highest in the summer.

In the past thirty years, programs to improve air **quality** have made **significant** progress in reducing air pollution in cities. Most of these air quality improvement programs have focused on getting **factories** to reduce the amount of

pollution they put into the air. New programs, however, target air quality on a smaller scale. They want to improve the quality of air in children's daily lives. A good example of this is a new type of "No Smoking" law. Its goal is to reduce secondhand smoke—cigarette smoke in the air that others breathe in.

More than 150 countries now prohibit smoking in enclosed public places such as workplaces. However, experts say that secondhand smoke is just as dangerous outside as inside. Some countries including Hungary, Iceland, India, Singapore, and Spain have banned smoking outdoors in places visited regularly by children. Smokers may have to pay fines for smoking in public outdoor recreation areas such as city parks, beaches, gardens, or playgrounds.

These laws have become quite popular internationally because people want to reduce the amount of secondhand smoke that children breathe. Others want to help the **environment** in general. Most want both. "Those of us living in an urban environment are constantly exposing ourselves to toxic **substances**," one city health official said. "I'm in favor of anything that cleans up our environment."

C. With a partner, discuss these questions about the reading.

1. Why are children more affected by air pollution than adults are?

2. What is different about the new "No Smoking" laws?

3. What have countries done recently to improve air quality?

D. Circle the answer that correctly completes the definition of the word. Look back at the article on page 67 to check your answers.

1. To have an <u>impact</u> on someone or something means to have ___.
   a. an effect
   b. an opinion

2. The <u>population</u> of an area is another way to say the ___ in that area.
   a. people
   b. children

3. To measure the <u>quality</u> of something means learning how ___ it is.
   a. big or small
   b. good or bad

4. When something is <u>significant</u>, it is ___ .
   a. important
   b. not important

5. A <u>factory</u> is a place where a company makes products in ___ quantities.
   a. large
   b. small

6. In the article, the <u>environment</u> refers to the ___ around us.
   a. businesses, factories, and offices
   b. air, water, and land

7. A <u>substance</u> is ___ that has special characteristics.
   a. an idea or plan
   b. a type of solid, liquid, or gas

E. Circle the word with a similar meaning to the underlined idiom.

The increasing number of children with breathing problems and diseases <u>paints a picture</u> of the quality of the air in urban areas.

a. influences
b. describes

F. Discuss these questions in a group. Share your answers with the class.

1. How do you feel about smoking outdoors? Do you think it is a problem? Why or why not?

2. Do you think that smoking increases the general air pollution in a city? Why or why not? Will banning outdoor smoking help a city's environment?

G. To help you understand the listening strategy, discuss the situation below with a partner, and answer the question.

Imagine that you are going to hear a lecture on the effects of air pollution on the environment. Which aspect of the lecture will help the class best understand the problem? Choose one.

a. an example of pollution   **c.** a definition of pollution
b. an explanation of pollution

LISTENING STRATEGY

Recognize Lecture Language for Explanations

Professors give explanations throughout lectures. They describe complex processes and ideas in ways that make them easier to understand.

Listen for the words and expressions that professors use to signal an explanation.

Expressions That Signal an Explanation

- Let me explain. . . .
- What I mean is . . .
- How does this work? . . .
- Let me spell this out. . . .
- Let me clarify. . . .
- Let's look at how this works. . . .
- I want to show you how . . . works. . . .
- Let me show you what I mean. . . .

H. Work with a partner to think of other expressions that signal an explanation. Write your examples here.

_____

_____

I. Read the excerpt from a lecture on the process of breathing. Underline and label the lecture language that signals each explanation and also the explanations.

Your lungs are complex organs. Let me explain what they do. They take a gas that your body needs to get rid of—carbon dioxide—and exchange it for a gas that your body can use—oxygen. In today's lecture we will take a close look at how your lungs work and how they keep your body's cells supplied with oxygen.

Your lungs' main job is to make oxygen available to your body and to remove other gases, such as carbon dioxide. This process is done 12 to 20 times per minute. Let me clarify how this process works. When you inhale air through your nose or mouth, air travels down the back of your throat (pharynx), passes through your voice box (larynx), and into your windpipe (trachea).

J. Listen to an excerpt from a lecture on ways people respond to pollution. Match the type of response to an example of the response.

____ **1.** respond personally   **a.** clean up rivers and beaches

____ **2.** become involved in environmental organizations   **b.** buy environmentally friendly office supplies

____ **3.** respond at work   **c.** ride a bike

K. Listen to the excerpt again. Write the lecture language that signals an explanation. Then listen again, and write down the explanation.

1. Idea: They change their personal worlds.

Explanation lecture language: _____

Explanation: _____

_____

2. Idea: They become involved in environmental organizations.

Explanation lecture language: _____

Explanation: _____

_____

3. Idea: Businesses are concerned.

Explanation lecture language: _____

Explanation: _____

_____

4. Idea: They purchase office supplies that are more environmentally friendly.

Explanation lecture language: _____

Explanation: _____

_____

NOTE-TAKING STRATEGY

Describe the Visuals Used in a Lecture

Professors often include visuals like pictures, charts, and graphs in lectures to clarify ideas. Make sure that you describe the visual in your notes and write down important information about it.

Excerpt and Visual from a Lecture

> You breathe in through your nose and mouth. The air travels down through a large tube in your throat called the windpipe. Then it moves through large and small tubes in your lungs called bronchial tubes or airways. The airways in your lungs look something like an upside-down tree with many branches.

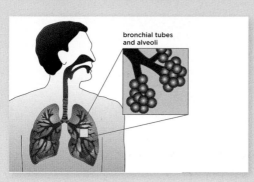

Representation of Visual in Notes

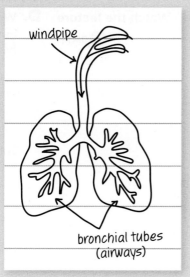

windpipe

bronchial tubes (airways)

Analyze the notes **A.** Read the excerpt, visual, and notes above. Then answer these questions in your notebook.

1. How complex is the student's drawing? Do you think it took a long time to draw?

2. What labels did the student use? Did she use enough labels?

3. Is the drawing complete enough to be useful to the student for studying? Why or why not?

Describe visuals **B.** Look at the professor's visual again. Read the professor's explanation of a part of the lungs called the alveoli. Take notes that describe the visual and the ideas. Include a simple drawing.

> The smallest airways end in the alveoli: small, thin air sacs that are arranged in clusters like bunches of balloons. When you breathe in, the alveoli expand as air rushes in to fill the lungs. When you breathe out, the alveoli relax and air moves out of the lungs.

Make predictions

See page 8

C. Before the lecture, think about everything you have learned and discussed on the topic of pollution. What do you expect to learn from the lecture? Write three predictions below. Compare your predictions with a partner.

1. _____

2. _____

3. _____

Watch the lecture

GO ONLINE

D. Watch the lecture, and take notes. Remember to listen for the lecture language that signals an explanation. Describe the graphics, and, if helpful, draw a simple picture of the visuals.

Topic:

Sulfur dioxide

Health problems caused by air pollution

Environmental problems caused by air pollution

Benefits of trees

E. Check the statement that best describes how well you were able to
recognize the lecture language.

I was able to recognize when the professor gave explanations ____.

a. all of the time   **b.** most of the time   **c.** sometimes   **d.** not often

F. Use your notes to answer these questions.

1. How is acid rain formed?

_____

_____

_____

_____

2. What is one of the biggest sources of sulfur dioxide? Why?

_____

_____

3. What are two of the ways that sulfur dioxide affects people and two
ways it affects nature?

_____

_____

_____

_____

4. What are three benefits of trees in the urban forest?

_____

_____

_____

G. Were you able to answer the questions in Exercise F using the
information in your notes? Compare and discuss your notes with a few
other students. Help each other fill in any missing information. Revise
your notes.

H. Work with a partner, and take turns. Review your notes from the lecture.
Then summarize the main points of the lecture for your partner. Talk for
2–3 minutes only.

ACADEMIC DISCUSSION STRATEGY	**Support Your Opinions**

Support Your Opinions

Your opinions are more interesting and persuasive when you support them with details, examples, personal experiences, and other information. Use expressions to indicate that you are supporting your opinions.

Expressions for Supporting Your Opinion

I think . . .

- Let me tell you why. . . .
- Let me give you an example. . . .
- and the reason is . . .
- because . . .
- for the following reasons: . . .

In my experience, that is/is not true. . . .

List more examples **A.** Work with a partner to think of other expressions for supporting your opinion. Write your examples here.

_____

_____

_____

B. In a group, read and discuss the questions below. Keep the conversation going until every student has had a chance to practice giving an opinion and supporting it. Use your own ideas and opinions or the ones given below.

1. Should people be allowed to drive cars without restrictions in major urban areas? Why or why not?

Yes	**No**
It's convenient.	It produces air pollution.
It gives you "alone time."	It produces noise
It's faster than public transportation.	pollution.
	It causes traffic jams.

2. Should people be allowed to smoke wherever they want?

Yes	**No**
People should have freedom of choice.	Smoking hurts others
Smokers shouldn't be punished for	(especially children).
having an addiction.	Smoking is messy.
It saves time (for example, smokers can	Smoke smells bad.
work rather than leave the building).	

C. Discuss these ideas with your classmates. Remember to use expressions for supporting your opinion.

1. Have you or anyone you know been affected by air pollution? Describe the effects.

2. Why don't people do more to help the environment? How can cities persuade people to reduce pollution?

3. Imagine that there is a large piece of undeveloped land for sale in your city. The city council is debating two proposals, or ideas, for what to do with the land:

   • Sell it for a lot of money to a developer who wants to build houses and businesses on it. The money from the sale would allow the city to clean up the river and create parkland along the riverbank.

   • Sell it to an environmental group for less money. This group wants to plant more trees on it and turn it into a nature preserve with hiking trails and camping areas.

   Discuss the two options and decide on one recommendation to give to city council.

4. Look back at your notes. What was another idea in the lecture that you found important or interesting? Tell the class why you think it is important or interesting, and ask for your classmates' opinions.

PRESENTATION STRATEGY

Open the Floor to Questions

It's important for the speaker to let the audience know when the presentation is finished. The speaker does this by first thanking the audience. Then because the audience might not have understood everything the speaker said, it's helpful to invite the audience to ask questions about the ideas in the presentation. This is called *opening the floor to questions*. At this point, the speaker must be certain he or she understands the question before answering it.

Open the floor to questions at the end of your presentation. Make sure you understand the question before answering it.

Check your comprehension

A. Watch a student give a presentation about pollution. Then answer these two questions.

1. What is the type of pollution?

_____

2. How does the pollution impact the environment?

_____

_____

Notice the conclusion

B. Watch the video again. Think about the information in the strategy box above. List two problems with the way the speaker opened the floor to questions.

_____

_____

_____

C. The student received some suggestions about his presentation and delivered it again. Watch the new presentation. List two improvements the student made to the way he opened the floor to questions.

_____

_____

_____

Expressions for Opening the Floor to Questions
- Thank you. Do you have any questions?
- Thank you for your interest. I'm happy to answer your questions.
- Thank you for listening. And now I'd like to take your questions.

Expressions for Checking That You Understand a Question
- Are you asking me . . . ?
- Do you mean . . . ?
- Let me see if I understand your question. It sounds like you're asking . . .

List more examples

D. Work with a partner to think of other ways to open the floor to questions. Write your examples in your notebook.

Practice opening the floor to questions

E. Stand in front of your group, and define one type of pollution. When you finish, open the floor to questions.

Practice the strategies for opening the floor to questions. Be sure you understand a question clearly before you answer it. After you finish, have your classmates give you feedback on how well you opened the floor to questions. Ask them these two questions:

1. What are two ways I effectively opened the floor to questions?

2. What is one way to improve how I opened the floor to questions?

Give a presentation

F. Prepare and deliver a presentation about environmental pollution.

Choose one type of environmental pollution such as:

Air	**Water**	**Land**
smoking	ocean acidification	soil erosion
smog	lead in drinking water	toxic waste

Research to learn about this pollution. In your presentation, describe:
- the problem

- where it occurs

- the impact on people, animals, plants, and/or the environment

- two solutions to the pollution

Give your opinion of the best solution. When you are finished, use the strategies for opening the floor to questions.

Before you prepare your presentation, review the ideas and vocabulary from this chapter.

A. Research an organization that works to protect the environment and reduce pollution.

Report Your Knowledge

Share your findings with the class. Include the following information:

• the name of the organization

• the type of pollution problems the organization attempts to solve

• two specific ways the organization works to protect the environment and reduce pollution

Remember to conclude your presentation by summarizing your most important information.

B. Work in a group. Go online, and research ways to reduce pollution in your everyday life.

Discuss the Ideas

Discuss any new ideas you find. Share ideas of how students can reduce pollution in their lives. Develop a list of suggestions for your classmates.

Report Your Knowledge

Share your suggestions with the class. Conclude by summarizing your most important ideas. Leave time for questions and answers.

C. Visit the USDA Web site to learn about healthy diets. Then do the activities below.

• Look at the USDA's new diet and exercise recommendations. What recommendations does the USDA have for a person of your age and level of activity?

• Compare your current diet and level of exercise with what the USDA recommends. Do you agree with the recommendations? Why or why not?

• Think about the changes you would have to make in your life to follow the USDA recommendations. How easy would this be for you? Do you plan to make the changes? Why or why not?

Report Your Thoughts

Share your results and answers with the class. Remember to conclude with a summary of your main ideas. Then open the floor to questions.

Unit Goals

CHAPTER 7
Learn about current trends in media use

Listening Strategy
• Recognize lecture language that signals important information

Note-Taking Strategy
• Highlight important ideas in your notes

Academic Discussion Strategy
• Connect your ideas to other students' ideas during the discussion

Presentation Strategy
• Refer to a chart or a graph during a presentation

CHAPTER 8
Learn about media literacy and stereotyping on television

Listening Strategy
• Recognize non-verbal signals for important information

Note-Taking Strategy
• Annotate your lecture notes during and after a lecture

Academic Discussion Strategy
• Remain focused during the classroom discussion

Presentation Strategy
• Use hand gestures to clarify words and ideas in a presentation

UNIT 4

Media Studies

media studies \\'midiə 'stʌdiz\\ The study of the processes by which information is exchanged

Think about the topic

A. Look at the picture of a person reading the news. Then discuss the questions below with a partner.

1. What are some traditional ways that people get the news every day?

2. What are some new ways that people get the news?

3. How do you get the news?

4. Imagine that you hear about a natural disaster such as a hurricane or an earthquake. What would you do to get news about it?

5. How would you compare the quality of the news today versus news in the past?

B. Read this article about some of the ways that news has changed.

The Nature of News

What do people mean by the term "news"? An editor once explained it this way: "If a dog bites a man, it's not news. If a man bites a dog, that's news." That statement suggests that unusual things make the news. Conflicts and events that are very recent are also news. When famous people do something, that's news, too.

The news **media** is undergoing tremendous change. For example, more and more people today have **access** to the Internet, where they can choose what type of news to look at. These days, people are choosing "news you can use." This means that rather than looking for **in-depth** news stories about events in the world, people want news about their own needs and concerns. People want **reliable** information about the traffic on the roads near their home, jobs they can apply for, or whether it's going to rain tomorrow. "News you can use" means **accurate** information that people can act on directly by taking a different route to work, knowing when to submit a job application, or by changing their weekend plans.

Another **feature** of today's news is its focus on analysis. In the past, the news gave people information about individual events. Today, people depend on the news to **get informed** about how individual events happen together to affect the world, their work, or their lives. As much as they want to know what's happening, they also want to know what it means for their lives. News reporters are constantly searching for groups of events that signal new trends. For example, through online news, word of major disasters spreads around the world within minutes of an event. As soon as that news is transmitted, people can find information about who has been affected and ways people can help. For example, within hours of the 2010 earthquake in Haiti and the 2011 tsunami in Japan, people all over the world knew about the events. Almost as quickly, you could read about international organizations that were helping, and how to contribute goods or money to help. This kind of news analysis helps people **keep up with** world events and better understand how to adapt to them or assist other people.

The new emphasis on practical news applies to every type of news medium—TV, **print** media, radio, and especially the Internet. With so many media choices, there is almost no limit to the amount of "news you can use."

C. Answer the questions about the article. Then discuss your answers with a partner.

1. What does the term *news you can use* mean?

_____

2. What is the benefit of today's focus on news analysis?

_____

3. What kind of news do reporters search for now? What is one example?

_____

D. Match the words in the reading with their definitions. Look back at the article on page 81 to check your answers.

____ **1.** media	**a.**	can be trusted
____ **2.** access	**b.**	find out about
____ **3.** in-depth	**c.**	TV, radio, newspapers, the Internet, as a group
____ **4.** reliable	**d.**	a way of entering or reaching
____ **5.** accurate	**e.**	with a lot of details
____ **6.** feature	**f.**	writing that is in books, magazines, and newspapers
____ **7.** get informed	**g.**	an important or noticeable part of something
____ **8.** print	**h.**	careful and exact

E. Circle the phrase with a similar meaning to the underlined idiom.

Reading the newspaper every day helps people <u>keep up with</u> international, national, and local events.

a. write down   **b.** continue to learn about   **c.** talk to people about

F. Discuss these questions in a group. Share your answers with the class.

1. When you pick up a newspaper or visit a news Web site, are you more interested in news about world events or "news you can use"? Why?

2. Which is more reliable, news in a newspaper or news on the Internet? Why do you think so?

G. With a partner, discuss three things that you have learned from the reading and from your discussions about the news.

1. _____

2. _____

3. _____

H. To help you understand the listening strategy, discuss the situation below with a partner, and answer the question.

During a lecture, the professor says, "Now, let me repeat that." What should you do?

a. Stop listening because you heard it already.

b. Listen carefully because the information must be important.

LISTENING STRATEGY

Recognize Lecture Language That Signals Important Information

During a lecture, a professor will often communicate that he or she is making an important point and that you should pay special attention to it. When this happens, be sure to write the information down.

Listen for the words and expressions that professors use to signal important information.

Expressions That Signal Important Information

- Listen to this: . . .
- This is important.
- You should write this down.
- Let me repeat that. . . .
- I'll say that again. . . .
- I want to point out that . . .
- It's important to note that . . .
- Pay attention to this: . . .
- I want you to notice that . . .
- The bottom line is . . .
- Here's the bottom line: . . .
- This will be on the test.

List more examples

I. Work with a partner to think of other expressions that signal important information. Write your examples in your notebook.

Recognize lecture language for important information

J. Read the two excerpts from a lecture about news media. Underline and label the lecture language that signals an important piece of information and also the information.

Excerpt 1

All right. So far, we've been saying that people depend on the news to get informed about how events happen. I want to point out that the kind of news they look for is news that affects their lives directly. They want to know what's happening, but they also want to know what it means for their lives.

Excerpt 2

So, earlier I mentioned the role of reporters in gathering the news. And we said this discussion can apply to print, television, radio, and even Internet news. It's important to note that reporters are now looking for trends to report as news in all kinds of places—in stores, in the workplace, and even in schools.

K. Listen to an excerpt from a lecture about the news. Match the first part of each sentence with the correct second part.

_____ **1.** The number of hours people are online is

_____ **2.** Getting the news on the Internet is

_____ **3.** More people are using the Internet

a. to get information about big events.

b. 12½ hours per week.

c. the third most popular Internet activity.

L. Listen to the excerpt again. Write down the lecture language that signals important information. Then listen again, and write down the important information.

1. Important information lecture language: _____

   Important information: _____

   _____

2. Important information lecture language: _____

   Important information: _____

   _____

3. Important information lecture language: _____

   Important information: _____

   _____

4. Important information lecture language: _____

   Important information: _____

   _____

5. Important information lecture language: _____

   Important information: _____

   _____

6. Important information lecture language: _____

   Important information: _____

   _____

NOTE-TAKING
STRATEGY

Highlight Important Ideas

Some ideas in a lecture are very important. These can be facts, research results, examples, or definitions. As you listen, highlight the important points in your notes by marking them.

Excerpt from a Lecture and Student Notes

There have been a number of recent studies on Internet use. The most recent study, from the University of Southern California, has the most accurate finding on Internet use. One important point they found is that people go online an average of 12 and a half hours per week. Another important finding was that getting the news was the third most popular activity on the Internet. I'd like to point out a significant but more recent finding—there was a large increase in the number of people going to the Internet for big event news . . . that means news about war, or deaths of important people. So the point I want to stress the most is that the Internet is now the preferred source for big, current news stories for many people.

Recent studies on Internet use
most recent—most accurate findings
Univ S. CA Int. use survey found
* people go online avg 12.5 hr/week
* getting news=3rd most popular activity
increase in # of Int. users for BIG EVENT news
war, deaths of important people, etc.
→ Internet = preferred source for big, current news

Analyze the notes **A.** Read the lecture excerpt and notes in the strategy box above. Then answer these questions.

1. What ways did the student use to highlight information? Give examples.

   _____

2. What is the most important point in the lecture?

   _____

B. Read this excerpt from a lecture on the changing nature of news. Take notes in your notebook. Highlight important information.

> I want to stress that the news people want today is practical news. For example, . . . and this is important, . . . they want information about the weather and they want reliable traffic information. These are both practical kinds of news. The Internet is particularly important here for two reasons, . . . now write this down: it's often easier for people to access the Internet than a newspaper, and there is so much more of this kind of practical news available on the Internet.

C. Before the lecture, think about everything you have learned and discussed on the topic of getting the news. What do you expect to learn from the lecture? Write three predictions below. Compare your predictions with a partner.

1. _____

2. _____

3. _____

D. Watch the lecture, and take notes in your notebook. Remember to listen for the lecture language that signals important information. Highlight important information as well.

E. Check the statement that best describes how well you were able to recognize the lecture language.

I was able to recognize important information ___.

a. all of the time   **b.** most of the time   **c.** sometimes   **d.** not often

F. Use your notes to answer these questions.

1. What trends do experts see in the way people get the news?

_____

_____

_____

2. Why did the professor mention the importance of young people?

_____

_____

_____

3. Why are people choosing to get news from the Internet?

_____

_____

_____

4. What are three negative aspects of getting news from the Internet?

_____

_____

_____

G. Were you able to answer the questions in Exercise F using the information in your notes? Compare and discuss your notes with a few other students. Help each other fill in any missing information. Revise your notes.

H. Work with a partner, and take turns. Review your notes from the lecture. Then summarize the main points of the lecture for your partner. Talk for 2–3 minutes only.

ACADEMIC DISCUSSION STRATEGY

Connect Your Ideas to Other Students' Ideas

During a discussion, you may have an idea that is related to something that someone else said. Use expressions to show that you understand how these ideas are connected and that you want to add your idea to the discussion.

Expressions for Connecting Your Ideas to Others' in a Discussion
- My idea is similar to Sam's.
- I disagree with what Sam said.
- As Sam already pointed out, . . .
- Going back to what Sam said before, I . . .
- Sam said . . . , and I'd like to add . . .

List more examples

A. Work with a partner to think of other expressions you can use to connect your ideas to others' in a discussion. Write your examples here.

_____

_____

_____

B. In a group, read and discuss the questions below. Keep the conversation going until every student has had a chance to practice using the language for connecting ideas. Use your own ideas or the ones given below.

1. What kind of information can you get on the Internet?

> **Possible Ideas**
>
> | | |
> |---|---|
> | news | health information |
> | shopping | weather |
> | sports | advice |
> | stock quotes | local activities |

2. Why is it important to get the news?

> **Possible Ideas**
> to help make decisions
> to be prepared for changes
> to know about the world
> to have something to talk about with friends

C. Discuss these ideas with your classmates. Remember to use the phrases for connecting your ideas to other ideas.

1. The lecture points out that Internet news is current, complete, and interactive. When have you found this not to be true? Give examples.

2. What is one other positive or negative aspect of Internet news that you have noticed?

3. In your experience, do you feel young people know enough about current world events? How is the media involved in this?

4. Look back at your notes. What was another idea in the lecture that you found important or interesting? Tell the class why you think it is important or interesting, and ask for your classmates' opinions.

PRESENTATION STRATEGY

Refer to a Chart or a Graph

Sometimes a speaker needs to help the audience understand complex information with numerical data and statistics. A speaker can show this information in a visual such as a chart or graph. The visual will help the audience understand the complex information. However, a speaker should not assume that the audience will immediately understand the visual and how it relates to the presentation. To speak effectively about visual images, the speaker can guide the audience by doing the following.

- Tell the audience what they will see before you show the visual.
- Help the audience understand how the information is organized.
- Focus the audience's attention on a specific point.
- Stand next to but not in front of the visual, so it is easy for the audience to see it.

Speak effectively about visual images to guide your audience.

Check your comprehension

A. Watch a student give a presentation about getting the news. Then answer these two questions.

1. What survey question did the student ask?

_____

2. What are two important findings of the survey?

_____

Notice how the speaker talks about a graph

B. Watch the video again. Think about the information in the strategy box above. In your notebook, list two problems with the way the speaker spoke about a chart.

C. The student received some suggestions about her presentation and delivered it again. Watch the new presentation. In your notebook, list two improvements the student made to how she referred to the chart.

PRESENTATION STRATEGY

Expressions for Speaking Effectively About a Chart or a Graph
- Now I'm going to show you a graph that shows . . .
- Along the left side, you can see . . .
- As you can see here . . .
- If you look across the top of the graph, . . .

List more examples

D. Work with a partner to think of other ways to refer to a visual. Write your examples in your notebook.

E. Work in a group. Below is a graph related to media use in the United States. The graph shows results of a survey about where people get their news.

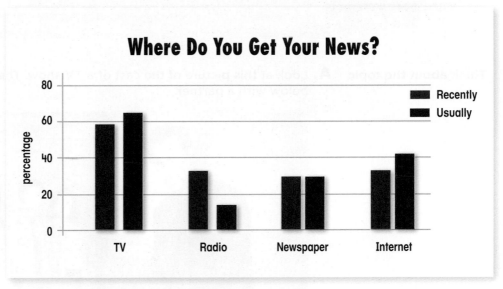

Where Do You Get Your News?

Stand in front of your group, and use the strategies to speak about the information in the graph.

After you finish, have your classmates give you feedback on how you refer to a graph. Ask them these two questions:

1. What are two ways I effectively speak about a graph?

2. What is one way to improve how I speak about a graph?

F. Prepare and deliver a presentation about how people get their news.

Interview at least ten people from two of these age groups: 18–29, 30–57, or 58 and up. Choose one of the following questions. Then make a graph of your results to show during your presentation.

1. How much time do you spend getting the news every day?

2. What sources do you go to for news?

3. How do you get the news about your local community?

4. Do you consider yourself well-informed about your local community?

In your presentation, give the topic and age groups you interviewed, tell the questions, show your graph, describe your findings, and give a possible explanation.

Before you prepare your presentation, review the ideas and vocabulary from this chapter.

STEP 1 Listen and Apply New Strategies

Think about the topic

A. Look at this picture of the cast of a TV show. Then discuss the questions below with a partner.

1. What type of TV show do you think these actors are on? Why do you think so?

2. Do you think you would like this TV program? Why or why not?

3. Why do people like to watch TV? What do TV programs offer them?

4. What types of TV shows do you enjoy watching?

5. Do you find TV to be a good representation of a culture and its values? Why or why not?

B. Read this article about common themes used in television programs.

Themes in Television Entertainment

Television gives viewers a wide range of entertainment choices. Or does it? When we look at the broad pattern of characters and plots, we can see that most television entertainment includes the same few favorite themes and messages. These can be summarized as follows:

Money. In the TV world, people usually have a lot of nice things: houses, cars, clothes. This sends a message that having a lot of nice things is normal and desirable. In advertising, we **take** this message **for granted**. Advertisers want to attract buyers to their product. Television programs are now delivering a similar message for similar reasons: They want to attract viewers to their shows. We see this in the number of programs featuring rich, beautiful **characters** living in homes and driving cars that a real person in their situation could not possibly afford.

Danger. The world, according to television, is a risky and dangerous place. Television programs such as police **dramas** show us a tremendous amount of violence and crime.

Respect. In TV life, people with professional jobs get more respect than people with service or manual jobs such as waitresses or factory workers. This is true in all kinds of programs, especially **comedy** shows.

Business. Businesspeople cannot be trusted, at least not on TV. In program after program, businesspeople cheat, lie, or use other people.

Fantasy. TV programs reflect a strong desire in viewers for **fantasy**. People like to forget **reality** for an hour and imagine worlds that do not exist, life on other planets, and life after death. Even shows that are not fantasy often try to include some piece of fantasy because they know it will attract viewers. An interesting **aspect** of fantasy programs is the way that they use people's natural fear of the unknown. Things that people cannot explain are usually presented as bad, dangerous, or evil.

Self-interest. People in the television world are extraordinarily interested in themselves. Many characters on TV think only about getting what they want. They are not **conscious** of other people's desires or needs. For example, one man tricks another man in order to take his job. He doesn't consider the other man's feelings or needs, or those of their coworkers. He wants that job, so he does anything to get it.

These common themes from television are seldom true in real life and usually involve **stereotypes** of people: the lazy janitor, the lying businessperson, the troubled teenager. These stereotypes can be funny, but they can also be insulting and untrue.

C. Fill in the chart with examples or supporting points from the reading. Then discuss your answers with a partner.

Common Themes on Television	Examples or Details
1. Having a lot of nice things.	Many programs with rich people/people living in homes/driving cars they can't pay for
2. The world is dangerous.	
3. Professional people deserve more respect than workers.	
4. Businesspeople are not honest.	
5. People have a strong desire for fantasy.	
6. People are only interested in themselves.	

D. Circle the answer that correctly completes the definition of the word. Look back at the article on page 93 to check your answers.

1. <u>Characters</u> are the ___ in a book, movie, or television show.

    a. people   **b.** locations

2. <u>Dramas</u> are movies or television programs that are ___.

    a. funny   **b.** serious

3. A <u>comedy</u> is a ___ kind of television program or movie.

    a. serious   **b.** funny

4. <u>Fantasy</u> is a situation that is ___.

    a. true   **b.** from the imagination

5. <u>Reality</u> is the way ___ really is.

    a. television   **b.** life

6. An <u>aspect</u> is one ___ of an idea, situation, or problem.

    a. part   **b.** example

7. To be <u>conscious</u> of something means to be ___ of something.

    a. a part   **b.** aware

8. <u>Stereotypes</u> are ___ and often untrue ideas about people or things.

    a. common   **b.** strange

E. Choose a phrase with a similar meaning to the underlined idiom.

Viewers take for granted that people in TV ads are not like real people.

a. accept without thinking about it   **c.** don't understand
b. prefer without really caring

Discuss the reading

F. Discuss these questions in a group. Share your answers with the class.

1. Do you agree with the writer that people watch television to forget about the reality of their lives? If you agree, is this a good thing or a bad thing? If you disagree, explain why you think people watch television.

2. Many of the ideas in the article talk about how television does not represent reality well. Do you think this is true? How do you feel about this?

Review what you know

G. With a partner, discuss three things that you have learned from the reading and from your discussions about themes in television.

Prepare for the listening strategy

H. To help you understand the listening strategy, discuss the situation below with a partner, and answer the question.

Imagine you are listening to a lecture and the professor stops talking and writes a word on the board. What should you do?

a. Review your notes.   **b.** Write the word down.

LISTENING STRATEGY

Recognize Non-Verbal Signals for Important Information

In addition to using words to tell you that a piece of information is important, professors use non-verbal signals—gestures and movement—to signal that something is important.

Watch for non-verbal signals about the importance of a point or idea, and write the information down.

Non-verbal Signals for Indicating That Something Is Important
- The professor writes down a piece of information.
- The professor projects the information on a slide.
- The professor uses gestures: uses hands, counts on fingers, pounds on the podium.
- The professor leans forward or moves toward the students.
- The professor pauses and looks at all the students.

List more examples

I. Work with a partner to think of other non-verbal signals that indicate an important point in a presentation. Write your examples in your notebook.

J. Look at the photos of a professor giving a lecture. Then read the three quotes from the lecture. Match the non-verbal signal with the idea the professor is talking about.

The professor says:

___ **a.** "Today we'll discuss three common stereotypes on TV. First, let's talk about gender stereotypes."

___ **b.** "Images of powerful men doing powerful jobs are in many programs on TV."

___ **c.** "The selection of TV programs seems extremely wide to average watchers, but not to the experts."

Watch the lecture

GO ONLINE

K. Watch an excerpt from a lecture about television characters. Match the first part of each sentence with the correct second part.

___ **1.** Almost all characters on TV   **a.** get hurt or injured.

___ **2.** TV characters rarely   **b.** are healthy.

___ **3.** Very few TV characters   **c.** are fat or unhealthy.

Notice non-verbal signals

GO ONLINE

L. Watch the excerpt again. Write down four of the non-verbal signals that the speaker uses to indicate important ideas. Then watch again, and write down the important idea.

1. Non-verbal importance signal: _____

    Important idea: _____

2. Non-verbal importance signal: _____

    Important idea: _____

3. Non-verbal importance signal: _____

    Important idea: _____

4. Non-verbal importance signal: _____

    Important idea: _____

NOTE-TAKING STRATEGY

Annotate Your Notes During a Lecture

Professors present a lot of information in one lecture, and you might not understand everything they say. It's important to write down the questions or difficulties you have in your notes and refer to these after the lecture.

Annotate your notes with questions or reminders to yourself of something you need to study after the lecture.

Annotated Notes

TV Themes
Health of chars on TV=useful for understanding power of TV
media (look up "media")
Almost all TV characters = healthy
even w/ shooting/car crash ???
Rarely get hurt
even w/o seat belts
(Re-read textbk chap. on this)
Eating=unhealthy
Too much food, candy, coffee
* Very few fat/unhealthy people Why is this possible?

Analyze the notes   **A.** Read the sample notes in the strategy box above. List the types of annotation used.

_____

_____

_____

_____

Make predictions

See page 8

B. Before the lecture, think about everything you have learned and discussed on the topic of television themes. What do you expect to learn from the lecture? Write three predictions below. Compare your predictions with a partner.

1. _____

2. _____

3. _____

Watch the lecture

GO ONLINE

C. Watch the lecture, and take notes in your notebook using annotation. Remember to pay attention to non-verbal signals for important information.

Assess your comprehension

D. Check the statement that best describes how well you were able to recognize the lecture language.

I was able to recognize when an idea was important ___.

___ most of the time   ___ sometimes   ___ not often

E. Use your notes to answer these questions.

1. What are three ways that the characters on TV differ from people in the real world?

   _____

   _____

   _____

2. What are some television stereotypes of men? Describe them.

_____

_____

_____

3. What is one television stereotype of women? Describe it.

_____

_____

_____

4. What are some concerns about the way TV presents the world and people?

_____

_____

_____

_____

Assess and revise your notes
See page 9

F. Were you able to answer the questions in Exercise E using the information in your notes? Compare and discuss your notes with a few other students. Help each other fill in any missing information. Revise your notes.

Summarize the lecture
See page 21

G. Work with a partner, and take turns. Review your notes from the lecture. Then summarize the main points of the lecture for your partner. Talk for 2–3 minutes only.

ACADEMIC DISCUSSION STRATEGY

Keep the Discussion Focused

During a discussion, students sometimes bring up ideas that are not closely related to the topic. In this situation, the other students should politely try to bring the discussion back to the original topic. Use expressions to keep the discussion focused.

Expressions for Keeping a Discussion Focused

- Could we go back to . . . ?
- I think we're getting off track.
- Maybe we should get back to the question.
- Let's get back on track.
- Maybe we could talk about that later.
- Let's stay focused.
- That's a good point, but for now let's stay with . . .

List more examples

A. Work with a partner to think of other expressions for keeping a discussion focused. Write your examples here.

_____

_____

_____

Practice keeping the discussion focused

B. In a group, read and discuss the questions below. Keep the conversation going until every student has had a chance to practice using the language for keeping the discussion focused. Use your own ideas or the ones given below.

1. When do you watch TV?

Possible Ideas

after waking up	during meals
before going to bed	when there is nothing to do
after work	when there is an important event

2. What do you like and dislike about television?

Possible Ideas

Like	**Dislike**
TV is a no-brainer.	TV has too many ads.
It's fun to look at beautiful people.	It has too many stupid characters.
It's a good way to learn languages.	It hurts my eyes.

Discuss the ideas in the lecture

C. Discuss these ideas with your classmates. Remember to use the phrases for keeping the discussion focused.

1. In your opinion, how do television programs show viewers a world that is different from reality? How do you feel about this?

2. How important is media literacy? Do you think it can really affect people's TV viewing habits and preferences? Why or why not?

3. If you could give advice to television writers on how to create a show that you and your friends would like, what would you suggest? What type of show would it be? What kinds of characters would it have? Why would people watch this show?

4. Look back at your notes. What was another idea in the lecture that you found important or interesting? Tell the class why you think it is important or interesting, and ask for your classmates' opinions.

PRESENTATION STRATEGY

Use Hand Gestures to Clarify Words and Ideas

The words a speaker uses in a presentation convey the most meaning. However, effective hand gestures can enhance the meaning of the words and ideas. Gestures can also help the audience recognize when an idea is important.

Use your hands to enhance what you're saying and to emphasize important ideas.

Check your comprehension

A. Watch a student give a presentation about stereotypes on television. Then answer these two questions.

1. What group of people does the student discuss?

_____

2. What is the student's opinion of television's portrayal of this group?

_____

Notice hand gestures

B. Watch the video again. Think about the information in the strategy box above. In your notebook, list two problems with the student's hand gestures.

C. The student received some suggestions about his presentation and delivered it again. Watch the new presentation. In your notebook, list two improvements the student made to his hand gestures.

Effective Hand Gestures

- Use hand gestures that match the idea you are talking about. For example, if you are saying, "There has been an increase," then move your hand upwards to represent an increase.
- When an idea is important, make a strong, intentional gesture. For example, clench your hand as you say the idea.
- Avoid using too many gestures; carefully decide which ideas need special emphasis or clarification. If you emphasize too many ideas, none will seem to stand out or have particular importance.

List more examples

D. Work with a partner to think of other effective hand gestures. Write your examples in your notebook.

Practice effective hand gestures

E. Stand in front of your group, and tell your classmates about one of your favorite television programs. Describe one of the themes in this program. Use the strategies for effective hand gestures.

After you finish, have your classmates give you feedback on your hand gestures. Ask them these two questions:

1. What are two ways I effectively used hand gestures?

2. What is one way to improve my hand gestures?

Give a presentation

F. Prepare and deliver a presentation about television portrayals of certain groups of people.

Choose one of these groups of people:

teenagers	students	people who have a particular job
children	men	fathers
older people	women	mothers

Watch a variety of television programs, and take notes of the negative or positive ways this group is portrayed.

In your presentation, describe the characteristics of the group you have chosen, give information about the TV shows you watched, and explain whether the TV shows use stereotypes or portray the people realistically. Give examples to support your explanation.

Before you prepare your presentation, review the ideas and vocabulary from this chapter.

A. Learn about ways that people are getting the news from blogs and micro-blogs such as Twitter and Weibo.

How does the news reported on these social networking sites differ from the news on traditional media such as newspapers and television?

Debate the Issues
Debate the pros and cons of getting the news from social media versus getting the news from traditional media.

B. The lecture compares the number and percentages of men and women, rich people, and professional people that are on TV to the number and percentages that exist in real life.

Listen and Take Notes
Interview people outside of class to see how closely they guess the numbers in each of the categories. Take notes on their answers.

Discuss the Results
Discuss your results in a group. How great is the difference? What accounts for the difference?

Present Your Conclusions
Share your results with the class, and present your conclusions for what accounts for the difference.

C. Compare news coverage in different media. Cut out a major news story from your local newspaper. Print out a story on the same topic from a Web site. Compare the two stories, and answer the questions.

1. Does the issue seem equally serious and important in both articles? If not, which medium makes the issue seem more important? What are some reasons for this?

2. Which article is written better? Why do you think so?

3. Which article do you think covers the story better? Why?

Present Your Comparison
Share the answers to the questions with your class. How do your answers compare with those of your classmates?

Unit Goals

UNIT

5

Linguistics

linguistics \lɪŋˈgwɪstɪks\ The study of language

Think about the topic   **A.** Look at the cartoon. Then discuss the questions below with a partner.

"Is everything all right, Jeffrey? You never call me 'dude' anymore."

1. Why do people use slang? Is slang necessary? Why or why not?

2. Does every language have slang?

3. Give some examples of slang in other languages.

4. Do you use slang? Who do you use it with?

5. In what contexts is slang appropriate? In what contexts is it not appropriate?

B. Read this blog about the purposes and value of slang in society.

Get Your Own Slang!

I'm standing outside Swenson's Internet Café in Kansas City, Missouri, and a group of teenagers is talking:

> Teenager 1: Yo, dawg, 's'up?
>
> Teenager 2: Chlllaxin'. You, Hom's?
>
> Teenager 1: Got mad stuff to do.
>
> Teenager 2: A-ight. Peace out.

I'm only ten years older than those kids, but I need one of them to translate for me. I've just entered a new culture, and all the rules, at least for language, are different here. The conversation seems **casual**, but I don't even know if they're being nice to each other or saying something **offensive**.

There's a new term for today's teenagers: The Millennial Generation. But you won't find such a formal phrase in the average teenager's vocabulary. What do they call each other? "Dawg," "BFF," or some other **informal** and sometimes strange **expression** to show that they belong to the same group?

Despite the way they look and speak, I think that today's teenagers are no different from any other generation. Teenagers have always used slang to identify with others in their age group and to show their independence from adults at the same time. Using slang gives their "club" its own language. When teenagers use slang, they're communicating their connection with each other, their group **identity**. These kids aren't just talking about what they're doing— they're connecting with each other by speaking the same language to talk about something that is probably only **relevant** to them.

Like teenagers of every generation, today's teenagers have many ways to establish their independent identity. They wear the same sorts of popular styles in clothing. Friends and larger **peer** groups travel in packs, listen to the same music, and all do the same activities. And yes, they speak whatever slang is currently **in style**.

Let the teenagers have their slang. We had ours, so it's fair. Being part of a group is important and "secret" languages are fun. The next time you hear teenagers speaking what sounds like a foreign language, just smile and say to yourself, "Cool."

C. With a partner, discuss these questions about the reading.

1. Why do teenagers use slang?

2. In what other ways do teenagers establish their own identity?

D. Match the words from the reading with their definitions. Look back at the article on page 107 to check your answers.

___ **1.** casual
   a. connected or related

___ **2.** offensive
   b. a person of the same age or in the same type of job

___ **3.** informal
   c. relaxed and friendly

___ **4.** expression
   d. the qualities of a group that make it different from others

___ **5.** identity
   e. unpleasant or insulting

___ **6.** relevant
   f. a group of words that go together

___ **7.** peer
   g. the opposite of formal

E. Circle the word with a similar meaning to the underlined idiom.

In the 1950s, most men had short hair. In the 1960s, long hair was <u>in style</u>.

a. attractive   **b.** unusual   **c.** fashionable

F. Discuss these questions in a group. Share your answers with the class.

1. Are teenagers the only peer group that uses slang? What other groups might have their own slang?

2. Is slang a good way for a group to establish its identity? Why or why not?

G. With a partner, discuss three things that you have learned from the reading and from your discussions about slang.

1. _____

2. _____

3. _____

H. To help you understand the listening strategy, discuss the situation below with a partner, and answer the question.

Imagine you are listening to a lecture. As the professor is making a point, she speaks louder. What does this mean?

a. The professor is angry with the students.

b. This point is important and the students should notice it.

LISTENING STRATEGY

Recognize Changes in Pronunciation

Professors often change the tone of their voice or their pronunciation to emphasize or clarify a word or idea. Recognizing these signals can help you catch important points more effectively.

Listen for pronunciation signals that professors use to clarify or emphasize a word or idea.

Pronunciation Signals to Emphasize One Word

Professors say the word
• more loudly
• more slowly
• with a higher pitch

Pronunciation Signals to Emphasize a Group of Words

Professors
• slow down as they say an important group of words
• pause before saying an important group of words
• pronounce each word separately or give each word special emphasis

List more examples

I. Work with a partner to think of other changes in pronunciation that signal important points. Write your examples here.

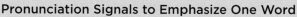

_____

_____

_____

Listen to the lecture

GO ONLINE

J. Listen to a short lecture about teenagers and slang. Match the first part of each sentence with the correct second part.

____ **1.** Teenagers today   **a.** worry about teenagers' slang.

____ **2.** Parents of teenagers   **b.** have fun with language.

____ **3.** Slang is a way to   **c.** have creative and interesting slang.

K. Listen to the short lecture again. As you listen, write down the important word or words. Then listen once more and write down the pronunciation signal that you heard.

> **Use these abbreviations for pronunciation signals:**
>
> **L** for louder
> **S** for slower
> **H** for a higher pitch
> **P** for a pause

1. Word or group of words _____

_____

Pronunciation signal _____

2. Word or group of words _____

_____

Pronunciation signal _____

3. Word or group of words _____

_____

Pronunciation signal _____

4. Word or group of words _____

_____

Pronunciation signal _____

5. Word or group of words _____

_____

Pronunciation signal _____

6. Word or group of words _____

_____

Pronunciation signal _____

NOTE-TAKING STRATEGY

Edit Your Notes after the Lecture

During a lecture, students take notes very quickly. It's possible to miss something, write something incompletely, or write something down incorrectly.

After the lecture, read through your notes quickly, and edit them while the lecture is still fresh in your mind.

The following is one student's notes from the short lecture on teenagers and slang from Exercises J and K on the previous pages.

a lot of   andard
↑Today's teenagers use slang + speak st↑ Engl.

teens use slang—then switch to ~~more~~ informal English

Switch again + use all kinds of technical language

    Ex: talk about computers

    something they have studied

They know when to use slang + when not to use it

Analyze the notes

A. Look at the student notes in the box above. List ways the student edited her notes.

_____

_____

_____

Edit the notes

B. Read this excerpt from the short lecture on teenagers and slang. Then look at one student's notes, and edit the notes to make them more complete.

> Some parents of teenagers worry when they hear their children use slang. They worry that their language is too informal or that other people won't understand them. They are also afraid that other people will think that their kids don't know how to speak English properly. We hear this all the time.

Parents worry when they hear slang.

Language is too formal

Other people won't understand them

They don't know how to speak English

Make predictions

See page 8

C. Before the lecture, think about everything you have learned and discussed on the topic of slang. What do you expect to learn from the lecture? Write three predictions below. Compare your predictions with a partner.

1. _____

2. _____

3. _____

Watch the lecture

 GO ONLINE

D. Watch the lecture, and take notes in your notebook. Remember to listen for the pronunciation signals used to clarify or emphasize a word or an idea.

E. Check the statement that best describes how well you were able to recognize the lecture language.

I was able to hear when words were being emphasized or clarified

__ most of the time   __ sometimes   __ not often

F. Use your notes to answer these questions.

1. Use your own words to explain the meaning of slang.

_____

_____

_____

2. Why do people use slang?

_____

_____

_____

3. What are three ways that slang is created? Explain each way.

_____

_____

_____

_____

4. Why is slang controversial?

_____

_____

_____

_____

G. Quickly re-read your notes and look for any information that is missing, incorrect, or incomplete. Edit your notes while the lecture is still fresh in your mind.

H. Work with a partner, and take turns. Review your notes from the lecture. Then summarize the main points of the lecture for your partner. Talk for 2–3 minutes only.

ACADEMIC DISCUSSION STRATEGY

Encourage Other Students to Participate in the Discussion

To create an interesting, thorough, and lively discussion, everyone in the group must contribute his or her ideas. But speaking isn't easy for everyone. You can help create a better discussion by asking other students to offer their ideas. Use expressions to politely encourage other students to participate in the discussion.

Expressions for Encouraging Other Students to Participate
- What does everyone else think?
- Has everyone shared their ideas?
- Lee, what do you think?
- Lee, can you add something here?
- Lee, how do you see the situation?
- What do you think, Lee?
- How about you, Lee? What do you think?
- We haven't heard from Lee yet.
- Let's hear from some others in the group.

List more examples

A. Work with a partner to think of other expressions for encouraging participation. Write your examples here.

_____

_____

_____

B. In a group, read and discuss the questions below. Keep the conversation going until every student has had a chance to practice encouraging other students to contribute to the discussion. Use your own ideas or the ones below.

1. Should people use slang?

   Possible Ideas

Yes	No
It helps express ideas better.	It's not correct language.
People can connect with each other.	People don't understand it.
It can be a fun, secret language.	It excludes people.

2. What are some of your favorite slang expressions?

   Possible Ideas

Good	Insults
cool	geek
sweet	airhead
awesome	poser

C. Discuss these ideas with your classmates. Remember to use the phrases for encouraging other students to participate.

1. What are the advantages and disadvantages of using slang for these different groups?

   - friends
   - older people
   - ethnic groups
   - co-workers
   - people living in the same region

2. Does it matter that slang sometimes breaks the rules of language? Why or why not?

3. Imagine a world in which slang did not exist. What would this world be like? For example, would teenagers and adults get along better because they always used the same language? Would people be more honest? Would you like to live in this world? Why or why not?

4. Look back at your notes. What was another idea in the lecture that you found important or interesting? Tell the class why you think it is important or interesting, and ask for your classmates' opinions.

PRESENTATION STRATEGY

Use Visuals That Combine Words and Pictures

Often a speaker uses a visual with words to show the topic, a list, a definition, or a question. Using a visual helps reinforce what a speaker says in a presentation. It shows the most important ideas in the presentation. When a visual combines words with a picture, the audience better understands and remembers the idea.

Visuals that combine words and pictures are most effective when the words

- are not an exact copy of what the speaker is saying
- highlight what the speaker is saying
- are easy for the audience to read
- are accompanied by a relevant picture that clarifies an important idea

Make visuals that combine words and pictures to help the audience understand and remember your ideas.

Notice the visuals

A. Look at the visual that one student used in his presentation about slang. Think about the information in the strategy box above. List two problems with the visual.

Ineffective Visual with Words and Pictures

 B. The student received some suggestions about his visuals and made new ones. Watch his revised presentation. List two improvements the student made to his visuals.

_____

_____

Making Effective Visuals with Words and Pictures
- Use a font size that is big enough for everyone in the room to read.
- Leave space between lines of words.
- Express each idea with a phrase, not a full sentence.
- Choose a picture that best clarifies an important idea, and place it where the audience can see the words and picture at the same time.

List more examples

C. Work with a partner to think of other ways to make effective visuals with words and pictures. Write your examples in your notebook.

Practice making effective visuals

D. Work in a group. Imagine you will present the information below. Make two visuals that combine words and pictures to help your audience understand and remember your presentation. Use the strategies for making visuals that combine words and pictures.

> Slang terms are often particular to a certain subculture. The slang term *pown* comes from the group of people who play video games. It started as an error in typing *own*, and is commonly spelled *pwn*. A video game player says "I powned you" or types "I pwned you" when he or she wins a video game and wants to brag about it. Now teenagers use it when they want to say they beat someone in a game or an argument.

After you finish, have your classmates give you feedback on your visuals. Ask them these two questions:

1. What are two ways I made effective visuals?

2. What is one way to improve how I make visuals?

Give a presentation

E. Prepare and deliver a presentation about a slang expression.

Choose a slang expression from your first language that you or people you know use. It could be borrowed from another language or not.

In your presentation, explain
- what the slang expression means
- how the expression was created
- how the slang expression is used

Use the strategies for making an effective visual that combines words and pictures.

Before you prepare your presentation, review the ideas and vocabulary from this chapter.

Think about the topic   **A.** Look at the map. Then discuss the questions below with a partner.

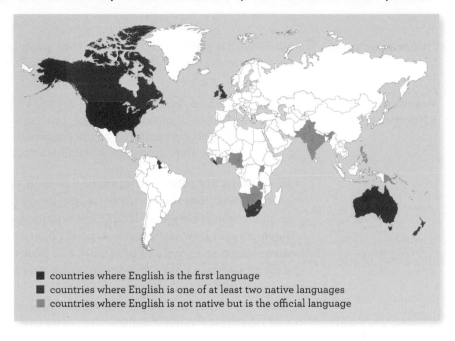

■ countries where English is the first language
■ countries where English is one of at least two native languages
■ countries where English is not native but is the official language

1. How many people in the world do you think speak English as a first language? As a second language? Give reasons for your guesses.

2. Which countries have English as one of several native languages? What are the other languages?

3. Which professions normally require a knowledge of English?

4. Think of people you know who speak English as a second language. Why did they learn English?

5. How do you think knowing English will benefit you in the future?

Read to build
background knowledge
See page 2

B. Read this article about how English is used in international business and politics.

International English

There is a **worldwide** trend toward international business—businesses in different countries coming together to trade goods and services. For example, Canada, the United States, and Mexico have all signed the North American Free Trade Agreement (NAFTA). This is an international agreement to lower **economic barriers** between the countries and end many limits on the buying and selling of goods.

Another example of this worldwide trend is the European Union (EU). The EU is an organization through which many countries in Europe have united economically and **politically**. The approximately 500 million people living in the European Union share common institutions and official policy agreements. These agreements make it easier for the **member** nations to do business together.

There are **significant benefits** for the countries involved in these agreements. The European Union, for example, has a much more powerful economy than that of the individual countries. Regions of Southeast Asia and Latin America have considered unified economies, as well.

International agreements such as NAFTA and the EU promote economic and political unity between countries. This means that member nations have to make decisions together about policies in many areas: agriculture, consumer affairs, business competition, the environment,

energy, transport, and trade. Language **plays a role**—an important role—in policy meetings. When the EU members come together to make decisions, many translators are needed. These translators keep Europe working smoothly in more than 20 different languages. This means there are more than 400 possible combinations of languages in any interaction within the EU.

With so many different languages, everyday conversations increasingly require a language that most of the people can already speak **fluently**—such as English. Although there is no official capital of the EU, Brussels serves as its unofficial headquarters. Most people in Brussels speak at least two or three languages, and English is increasingly the common language in any gathering of more than a few people. This situation is not **unique**. English is also used in many NAFTA meetings and other international gatherings around the world. The increased need for English in political circles is expected to continue a trend that has existed for years: using English for day-to-day business exchanges.

As more and more countries come together for political or business purposes, the need for a common language will only increase. Based on current trends, English seems to be the obvious choice.

Check your
comprehension

C. With a partner, discuss these questions about the reading.

1. What are two examples of the trend toward international business?

2. What is a benefit of countries making international agreements?

3. Why is English being used in EU meetings more and more often?

D. Circle the answer that correctly completes the definition of the word. Look back at the article on page 119 to check your answers.

1. Something that is <u>worldwide</u> is _____ in the world.

   a. everywhere   **b.** in a few places

2. <u>Economic barriers</u> are _____ that prevent countries from doing business with other countries.

   a. rules about language   **b.** rules about money

3. Something that is <u>political</u> has to do with the _____ of a country.

   a. language   **b.** government

4. A <u>member</u> of an organization is a _____ that belongs to a bigger group.

   a. individual person or group   **b.** set of rules

5. When something is <u>significant</u>, it has an _____ effect or influence.

   a. important   **b.** unimportant

6. A <u>benefit</u> is the _____ that you get from something.

   a. problem   **b.** advantage

7. To be <u>fluent</u> in a language means that you can speak it _____

   a. at a high level   **b.** at a low level

8. When something is <u>unique</u>, it is _____

   a. different and special   **b.** typical and good

E. Circle the phrase with a similar meaning to the underlined idiom.

Language, politics, and culture all <u>play a role</u> in international agreements.

a. are involved   **b.** are not present

F. Discuss these questions in a group. Share your answers with the class.

1. Why do international organizations like to have a common language?

2. Why do you think English is often the language chosen?

G. With a partner, discuss three things you have learned so far about the use of English in international organizations.

H. To help you understand the listening strategy, discuss the situation below with a partner, and answer the question.

Imagine that you are in a college class getting ready to listen to a two-hour lecture. Make a list of the listening strategies that you

feel confident using: _____

need to work on: _____

find the most helpful: _____

LISTENING STRATEGY

Review the Listening Strategies

Using the listening strategies in this book will help you better understand the topic, organization, and important points of your lectures.

Review the listening strategies to be sure you can use them effectively.

Review listening strategies

I. Look back at the strategies that have been presented in this book. Review them by giving some examples of lecture language for each one.

See page 5

1. Listen for the topic of a lecture _____

_____

See page 17

2. Listen for the big picture of a lecture _____

_____

See page 31

3. Listen for transitions in a lecture _____

_____

See page 43

4. Listen for definitions in a lecture _____

_____

See page 57

5. Listen for examples in a lecture _____

_____

See page 69

6. Listen for explanations in a lecture _____

_____

See page 83

7. Listen for important information in a lecture _____

_____

J. Listen to this short lecture on the business of teaching English worldwide. Match the first part of each sentence with the correct second part.

___ **1.** English is taught in   **a.** trained and untrained teachers.

___ **2.** English is taught by   **b.** English speaking countries.

___ **3.** Ideally, English is learned in   **c.** schools, businesses, and governments.

K. Listen to the short lecture again. Write down the lecture language. Then listen again, and write down the information that follows each instance of lecture language.

1. Topic lecture language: _____

Topic: _____

_____

2. Big picture lecture language: _____

_____

3. Transition lecture language: _____

New idea: _____

_____

4. Definition lecture language: _____

Definition: _____

_____

5. Example lecture language: _____

Example: _____

_____

6. Explanation lecture language: _____

Explanation: _____

_____

7. Importance lecture language: _____

Important information: _____

_____

Review the Note-Taking Strategies

Using the note-taking strategies in this book will help you better recall the important information in your lectures when you study.

Review the following note-taking strategies to be sure you can use them effectively.

- Write the most important words
- Use an informal outline
- Summarize the lecture
- Use symbols to represent words and ideas
- Use abbreviations to represent longer words
- Use a visual form
- Describe the visuals used in a lecture
- Highlight important ideas
- Annotate your notes during a lecture
- Edit your notes after a lecture

Review note-taking strategies

A. Read this excerpt from a lecture on the trend toward the use of English in international business. Then, look at one student's notes from the lecture (See page 124). Identify which seven note-taking strategies the student has used, and write them in your notebook. Give at least one example for each strategy.

I'd like to focus today on how decisions get made between members of trade groups like the North American Free Trade Agreement, which is referred to as NAFTA, and the European Union, which is commonly referred to as the EU. All the member nations of trade groups like NAFTA and the EU have to make decisions together about a variety of policies. They have to agree on policies that affect things like agriculture, consumer affairs, business competition, the environment, energy, transport, and trade. You get the picture? All these decisions get made in policy meetings.

Language plays a role—an important role—in all these policy meetings. Let me give you an example of what I mean by the importance of language. Currently, the number of member nations is 27—that is 27 different countries with almost the same number of languages. So, you can imagine that when the EU gets together to make decisions, a large number of translators is needed. These translators keep these policy discussions happening by offering translation into more than 20 different languages. That is what happens at official meetings in Brussels, the headquarters of the European Union.

Decision making for trade groups

      ex.   North Am. Free Trade Agreement (NAFTA)

              European Union (EU)

Policy meetings:

      make decisions about:

          agriculture

          consumer affairs

          business competition

          environment + policy energy

          transportation + trade

    * Language plays imp. role @ policy meetings

          # of countries @ meetings = 27

          # of diff languages > 20 languages for translation

              ——check what these are

Make predictions
See page 8

B. Before the lecture, think about everything you have learned and discussed on the topic of global English. What do you expect to learn from the lecture? Write three predictions below. Compare your predictions with a partner.

1. _____

2. _____

3. _____

Watch the lecture

GO ONLINE

C. Watch the lecture, and take notes in your notebook. Remember to listen for all the lecture language that you have learned.

Assess your comprehension

D. Check the statement that best describes how well you were able to recognize the lecture language.

____ I was able to recognize most of the lecture language.

____ I was able to recognize some of the lecture language.

E. Use your notes to answer these questions.

1. How many native speakers of English are there in the world? How many people speak some English?

   _____

   _____

   _____

2. What two trends have an influence on the growing use of English globally?

   _____

   _____

3. What four points of view about the spread of English are presented in the lecture? Explain them.

   _____

   _____

   _____

   _____

4. Some people fear the worldwide spread of English. What are two things that they fear might happen?

   _____

   _____

   _____

Assess and edit your notes
See pages 9 and 111

F. Were you able to answer the questions in Exercise E using the information in your notes? Compare and discuss your notes with a few other students. Help each other fill in any missing information. Edit your notes.

Summarize the lecture
See page 21

G. Work with a partner, and take turns. Review your notes from the lecture. Then summarize the main points of the lecture for your partner. Talk for 2–3 minutes only.

ACADEMIC DISCUSSION STRATEGY

Bring the Group to a Consensus

A consensus is an agreement among a group of people. Student study groups sometimes have to come to a consensus on one point of view or idea and present it to the whole class. To do this, the members of the group need to compare ideas, discuss them, then choose or compromise on one. Use expressions to help bring the group to a consensus.

Expressions for Coming to a Consensus in the Discussion

- Does everyone agree?
- So, is everyone satisfied with this?
- Does anyone have anything to add?
- Let's take a vote. Raise your hand if you agree with this idea.
- We're going to have to compromise. Maria, how strongly do you feel about . . . ?
- What can we all live with?

List more examples

A. Work with a partner to think of other expressions for coming to a consensus. Write your examples here.

_____

_____

_____

B. In a group, read and discuss the questions below. Keep the conversation going until every student has had a chance to practice coming to a consensus. Use your own ideas or the ones below.

1. What are the three best ways to learn English?

   Possible Ideas

   watch TV   take a grammar class
   make friends with native speakers   read in English

2. Why is it important to learn English? Give the three top reasons.

   Possible Ideas

   to listen to pop music   to earn more money
   to get a job   to use the Internet

C. Discuss these ideas with your classmates. Remember to use the phrases for coming to a consensus.

1. Which opinion about the spread of English do you agree with? Why?

2. In the lecture, the professor says that the main language used on the Internet is English. When you use the Internet, do you only visit English language Web sites, or do you visit Web sites that use other languages? Explain your answer.

3. Imagine there is a group of businesses that would like to make a trade agreement. Many languages are represented in the group: Mandarin, Spanish, English, Arabic. The group will do business equally in all regions. Is a common language necessary? If so, which language? If not, describe how multiple languages could work.

4. Look back at your notes. What was another idea in the lecture that you found important or interesting? Tell the class why you think it is important or interesting, and ask for your classmates' opinions.

PRESENTATION STRATEGY

Pace Your Speech

It's easy for a speaker to speak too quickly when delivering a presentation, especially if he or she is nervous. A fast speaking pace can make it difficult for the audience to follow the ideas in a presentation. Making frequent, brief pauses throughout a presentation slows down the rate of speech so the audience can follow the speaker's ideas. Therefore, it's important to know where and how often to pause.

As you speak, pace your speech by grouping your words and pausing to help the audience follow.

Check your comprehension

A. Watch a student give a presentation about the use of English in another country. Then answer these two questions in your notebook.

1. What is the name of the country?

2. How is English used in this country?

Notice the pacing

B. Watch the video again. Think about the information in the strategy box above. List two problems with the way the student paces her speech.

_____

_____

 C. The student received some suggestions about her presentation and delivered it again. Watch the new presentation while reading the transcript of the presentation. Mark with a slash (/) the places where the student pauses. In your notebook, list two improvements the student made to her pacing.

> Good afternoon, everyone. I grew up in Mexico, so that's the country I want to tell you about. Here's Mexico on a map. You know, when I was growing up in Mexico, I started learning English before I even started my first year of elementary school. Which was great. All my friends and I knew some words in English, and we would use them while we were playing.
>
> So today I'd like to tell you about English in Mexico. English is used in two important ways: in education and in business. Children begin learning English when they are very young, and many classes in the private colleges are taught in English. English is also used in business because Mexico does a lot of international business in the United States and in Canada. Therefore, it is necessary to know English if you work in a company that does business outside of Mexico.

Strategies for Effective Pacing
- Pause at the end of a phrase.
- Pause at the end of a clause.

List more examples | **D.** Work with a partner to think of other ways to pace your speech. Write your examples in your notebook.

Practice effective pacing | **E.** Stand in front of a group of classmates. Tell your group why you are learning English and how you will use English in your future.

To prepare, write out what you will say in full sentences. Mark the places where you should pause. Practice the strategies for pacing your speech.

After you finish, have your classmates give you feedback on your presentation. Ask them these two questions:

1. What are two ways I effectively paced my speech?

2. What is one way to improve how I pace my speech?

Give a presentation | **F.** Prepare and deliver a presentation giving your opinion of the role of English in a country you are familiar with.

English is used for different reasons in different countries. For example, in many countries, English is the language used in business, education, entertainment, or technology.

Do research to find out where and how English is used in a country of your choice.

Address the following in your presentation:

- Describe where and how English is used. Coordinate with classmates who are also talking about that country, and choose one area (e.g., business or entertainment) for each classmate to focus on.

- Give your opinion about how English is used. In what ways is the use positive or negative? Use supporting examples from your personal experience and/or observations.

- Give your opinion about changes (if any) you would like to see in the way English is used in the country. Explain your main ideas.

Use the strategies for pacing your speech.

Before you prepare your presentation, review the ideas and vocabulary from this chapter.

A. Discuss the controversy over teaching slang to students.

Some English teachers teach slang to their students. Others insist on teaching proper English.

Discuss Pros and Cons
As a class, discuss the pros and cons of teaching slang in English classes. Then divide into two groups. One group will prepare to debate in favor of teaching slang. The other group will prepare to oppose teaching slang.

Present Your Side
Use your strongest evidence to debate your side of the controversy. Be sure to pace your speech so that you sound confident and your ideas are clear to the audience.

B. Conduct interviews about the spread of English.

Listen and Take Notes
Interview at least three people from a non-English speaking country. Find out their opinion about the spread and use of English in their home country.

Discuss the Results
In a group, discuss the results of your interviews. Also, compare your interview results to the opinions discussed in the Chapter 10 lecture.

C. Research different types of slang.

There are many Web sites that present the slang used by different groups of people. Go online and find three categories of slang that are new to you. For each type of slang, write down the group that uses the slang and three good examples of it.

Present Your Research
Make sure the slang is appropriate to a school environment. Use the most appropriate information to develop a word visual with the information you gather in your research. Present your categories and examples to your class. Be sure to tell your classmates where you found the information.

ABOUT THE AUTHORS

PEG SAROSY

Peg Sarosy is an Academic Coordinator at the American Language Institute at San Francisco State University. She previously taught at San Francisco State University in the ESL program and the Design and Industry department. She also taught academic preparation at the University of California, Berkeley intensive English program and was a USIS Teacher Trainer in the Czech Republic. She has a master's degree in TESOL from San Francisco State University. Peg is co-author of *Lecture Ready 1* and *Lecture Ready 2* and a series editor for *Lecture Ready 3*.

KATHY SHERAK

Kathy Sherak is Director and Academic Coordinator at the American Language Institute at San Francisco State University. She previously taught in San Francisco State University's ESL program and was a Fulbright Teacher Trainer in Italy. She is the author of the *Grammar Sense 3 Teacher's Book* from Oxford University Press. She has a master's degree in TESOL from San Francisco State University. Kathy is co-author of *Lecture Ready 1* and *Lecture Ready 2* and a series editor for *Lecture Ready 3*.

Notes